THE AMERICAN IRISH AND IRISH NATIONALISM

A Sociohistorical Introduction

SEAMUS P. METRESS

The Scarecrow Press, Inc.
Lanham, Md., & London

SCARECROW PRESS, INC.

Published in the United States of America
by Scarecrow Press, Inc.
4720 Boston Way
Lanham, Maryland 20706

4 Pleydell Gardens, Folkestone
Kent CT20 2DN, England

British Cataloguing-in-Publication Information Available

Library of Congress Cataloging-in-Publication Data

Metress, Seamus P.
The American Irish and Irish nationalism : a sociohistorical
introduction / Seamus P. Metress.
p. cm.
Includes bibliographical references (p.   ) and index.
1. Irish Americans—Politics and government. 2. Nationalism
—Ireland—History. 3. Ireland—Politics and government—20th
century. 4. Northern Ireland—Politics and government—1969–
5. Ireland—Politics and government—1837–1901.   I. Title.
E184.I6M48 1995 973'.049162—dc20 95-31615 CIP

ISBN 0-8108-3059-0 (cloth : alk. paper)

⊖™ The paper used in this publication meets the minimum requirements of
American National Standard for Information Sciences—Permanence of
Paper for Printed Library Materials, ANSI Z39.48–1964.
Manufactured in the United States of America.

This work is dedicated to Joseph McGarrity of Philadelphia and Michael Flannery of New York, two Irish immigrants from counties Tyrone and Tipperary who spent most of their lives organizing and leading Irish-Americans involved in the struggle for freedom in Ireland.

Contents

Acknowledgments

I would like to acknowledge the invaluable assistance of Joanne Hartough and the interlibrary loan staff at the University of Toledo Library. They helped me to obtain by loan all items not available to me directly. This allowed me to directly examine each item that is cited in the bibliography. I would also like to thank my research assistant, Donna Johnston, who entered the material into the computer, proofread it, offered valuable suggestions and structured the final form. She is highly motivated, creative and very able.

Introduction

This work has been developed as a guide to the literature that documents the involvement of the American Irish in Irish national liberation struggles. It is an attempt to structurally organize and briefly annotate the available scholarly and popular literature on the subject. It is hoped that this work will be of value to those working in the area of ethnic studies, political science, popular culture and social history.

A brief historical introduction to the development of Irish Nationalism among the American Irish is included to provide a chronological framework for the main body of the work, the annotated bibliography.

Terminology has significant political connotations in the part of Ireland occupied by Britain today. Ulster is a term used primarily by pro-British loyalists, but is incorrect historically. The six northeastern counties are only part of the historic Ulster which included 3 counties now in the Republic of Ireland, Cavan, Monaghan, and Donegal. "Northern Ireland" is used primarily by the British but Nationalists do not like the term because it confers legitimacy on the statlet which many do not recognize. It is also geographically incorrect since the northernmost part of Ireland is in the county Donegal which is part of the Republic of Ireland which is often referred to as the south. Nationalists refer to the area as the six counties, or Northeast Ireland the latter of which is geographically incorrect since county Fermanagh is most certainly not in the northeastern portion. We will refer to the area as northern Ireland to avoid confusion for people not familiar with the political connotations, although the adjective northern will be presented in small case in order to highlight the contentious nature of such usage.

Part I
The American Irish and Irish Nationalism:
A Brief Introduction

For eight hundred years Ireland has been to some extent occupied and controlled by Britain. During this period both local and national resistance to British rule has been a regular occurrence. In 1921 twenty-six of Ireland's thirty-two counties won independence after the Anglo-Irish War. However, six of Ireland's counties remained under British control. In these six counties, known more commonly as Northern Ireland, intense resistance to the British presence has continued until this time. Although since late August of 1994 a ceasefire has emerged in hopes of working out a peaceful resolution to the conflict.

Irish-Americans have a long history of involvement in the struggle for Irish freedom. The nature of the Irish-American role and reasons why they became involved varied from one time period to the next. Organized participation dates back to the days of Daniel O'Connell's Repeal Movement of the 1840's and continues to the present day struggle in northern Ireland.

This paper will describe the nature of the Irish-American participation through time and propose a sociohistorical model to explain why the phenomenon has had such great longevity. The periods of Irish-American participation can be divided into the following:

1. From the Repeal and Young Ireland Movements to the Fenians
2. The Fenians to the Land War
3. The Land War to the Fall of Parnell
4. The Fall of Parnell to 1916
5. The Easter Rising through the Civil War
6. The Civil War to Civil Rights
7. Civil Rights to the Present.

Repeal and the Young Irelanders

In the 1840's Daniel O'Connell, after successfully forcing the British into a limited Catholic Emancipation Act in 1829, set his sights on the repeal of the Act of Union between Great Britain and Ireland. He wanted home rule with an Irish parliament but within the British empire. The repeal movement enlisted great numbers of Irish-Americans and repeal clubs were founded in almost every state. These clubs raised thousands of dollars and pressured politicians. Prominent American politicians, either by personal choice or in order to influence the growing Irish vote, spoke out on repeal. President Tyler's son Robert became the national repeal movement's leader. He once said, "All I know is that I love Irishmen and hate tyranny in every form" (Fleming 1979). Presidents Polk, Tyler and Buchanan nominally supported repeal while Governor Seward of New York and Horace Greeley of *The New York Herald* were outspoken supporters.

In the 1840's two Irish-American repeal conventions were held. At the same time Irish-American agitations were countered by the pro-British stance of the Know-Nothing Movement. The Know-Nothings, who disliked the Irish politically and religiously, viewed the repeal agitation as exhibiting loyalty to a foreign land and thus un-American.

In 1842 O'Connell urged Irish-Americans to join the abolitionists and refused to accept donations from southern groups that supported slavery. Many Irish-Americans disliked this attack on American institutions and values by a foreigner, even if he was Irish. Irish-born Archbishop John Hughes of New York said, "I am no friend of slavery but I am less friendly to any attempt of foreign origin to abolish it" (Fleming 1979). Irish-Americans were very loyal to the land that had allowed them to escape British tyranny and would not tolerate criticism of it, even by one of their own. The issue of O'Connell's support for the abolitionists destroyed the repeal movement.

In the midst of the great starvation the Young Ireland Movement rose to some prominence in Ireland. The Young Irelanders emphasized cultural nationalism and revived the memories of the rebels of 1798 and the united Irishmen who unsuccessfully tried to promote a non-sectarian revolution against British rule.. The movement also included a faction that supported violence to obtain freedom. They openly split with O'Connell over the promotion of open insurrection. Irish-Americans reacted by organizing repeal confederation meetings in Washington and New York that set up a directory to raise funds for the Young Irelanders. In August of 1848 a huge rally in New York to raise funds for weapons included a $500 contribution from Archbishop Hughes. However, in Ireland the movement was hampered by its mainly middle-class constituency and the fact that the Irish masses were weakened by the effects of the famine. A brief revolt was crushed ruthlessly by the British and Irish-Americans' hopes were quickly dashed. This experience seemed to convince Archbishop Hughes and other clergy that the rhetoric of revolution could not be trusted and they vowed never again to be distracted by it. Many Young Irelanders did come to America and brought with them the literature of cultural nationalism. They developed Celtic myths and stories to counter the WASPs and make the Irish feel that they were as good as anyone. The Young Irelanders frequently clashed with the Church hierarchy and Irish machine politicians over support for revolution and the corrupt aspects of party politics. It would seem that the liberal idealism of the Young Irelanders was blunted by Irish-American pragmatic political realism.

The Young Irelanders did establish the ideological basis for Irish-American support of revolution in Ireland. The priest might hold sway in matters religious and the Democratic Party in politics but the Young Irelanders - through cultural nationalism - spoke for their heritage and a free and independent Ireland. The work of the Young Irelanders intensified hatred of Britain and provided the literary and historical inspirations to carry on the struggle.

In the 1840's and 1850's Irish-Americans attempted to interfere in Anglo-American relations. During the 1844-46 Oregon boundary dispute the Irish were warhawks, in the Crimean War (1853-56) they supported the czar, and they supported Spain's claim to Gibraltar. Throughout the 1850's the Irish hoped that Napoleon III (Louis Napoleon) would free Ireland and their Irish-American allies concurred.

The Fenians to the Land Wars

In the mid-1850's the Irish-Americans moved toward another approach to freeing their homeland. In 1856, John O'Mahoney and Michael Doheny founded the Emmet Association which was changed into the Fenian Brotherhood in 1858. The Fenians were a secret society dedicated to armed revolution and the establishment of a Republic of Ireland. At the same time in Ireland (1858) James Stephens founded the Irish Republican Brotherhood (IRB). The two organizations were to co-ordinate efforts on both sides of the Atlantic that would lead to revolution.

The American Fenians were well organized but infiltrated by spies. They were attacked by many Catholic priests and bishops because they were a secret society with an oath of loyalty. The church in Ireland as well as the United States feared that Fenianism was related to the anti-clerical movements popular at the time in Europe.

The Fenian organization eventually became public and imitated the American government with a president, senate and a house of delegates. The movement was divided by dissension and factionalism into two groups. One group included the men of immediate action led by Colonel William Roberts who wanted to use ex-civil war veterans to attack the British empire in Canada. The other faction, led by John O'Mahoney, James Stephens and John Devoy, wanted to send money, equipment and men to Ireland. In 1866 some of the Fenians invaded Canada near Buffalo and after some initial success were defeated. Later invasions from Vermont and the Dakotas also failed. In Ireland the Fenians were constantly at odds with the church and a showdown in 1861 pitted Cardinal Cullen against the Fenians. Terence McManus, a Young Irelander who died in California, was brought home to Ireland to be buried. His body had already been carried by train across the United States complete with stops for viewing, so emotions were building. In Dublin, the Cardinal refused to allow a church burial so the IRB waked him at the Mechanics Institute. The Fenians scored a great psychological victory as 50,000 people marched behind the coffin to Glasnevin Cemetery in Dublin and a Mayo priest, Patrick Lavelle, buried him.

The Fenian Rising in Ireland during February/March 1867 failed militarily because of bad weather, poor timing and British infiltration which led to the jailing of some of the best leaders. Brave risings consisting of attacking the RIC (Royal Irish Constabulary) barracks occurred in Kerry, Cork, Tipperary, Limerick, Dublin and Clare. Later in England the executions of Allen, Larkin and O'Brien, who allegedly had accidently killed a police officer while trying to free two Fenian prisoners from a prison van, united the Irish people and in some cases even the church. "God Save Ireland," a song written about the Irish nationalists by T.D. Sullivan, became an unofficial national anthem.

In 1870 British pressure in Rome led to the pope condemning the IRB, but the Irish people for the most part resented his meddling in Irish affairs. Though militarily a failure the Fenians provided a spirit and ideology that has remained important even today. In the northeast of Ireland revolutionary nationalists are referred to as "Fenian bastards" by the British and their local loyalist supporters.

Back in America the demise of the Fenian Brotherhood in 1867 resulted in the founding of the Clan na Gael by Jerome Collins. The Clan na Gael attempted to avoid the mistakes of the Fenians by remaining very secret. From 1871 on it was to become dominated by John Devoy who led them into a formal agreement with the IRB in 1877. Clan na Gael attracted many prominent American leaders, especially labor leaders and politicians as well as many churchmen. Labor leaders like T.V. Powderly were especially active and old labor archives are a rich source of Clan na Gael history. Between 1876-81 they funded John Holland's research on the submarine with about $60,000 in hopes of using it against British ships.

The Land League to the Fall of Parnell

John Devoy, the Clan na Gael leader, wanted to build a link with the Irish masses. He found his opportunity when Michael Davitt, an Irish revolutionary, toured the United States. Davitt was converted to what Clan na Gael called their "New Departure Politics." New Departure consisted of a strategy that included the continued pressure of the Irish Parliamentary Party for the home rule issue. At the same time the Clan would prepare for revolution by recruiting and radicalizing the masses. The radicalizing of the masses would concentrate around:

1.   Fair rent agitation,
2.   Tenants' right to sell their interests in the land if they decided to leave or were evicted,
3.   Complete abolition of the landlord system with a peasant proprietorship.

Finally in 1882 Charles Stuart Parnell would demand home rule and when the British refused it would be the signal for a revolution of the now expectant masses.

Davitt returned to Ireland and founded the Land League of Mayo to agitate for land reform. This led to the founding of the National Land League, with Davitt at its head, which used the boycott to demand the end of landlordism. The movement attracted immediate massive support. It was largely non-violent in tone, but the old tradition of agrarian violence was never distant. Davitt resigned as head of the National Land League and let Parnell take his place.

In America The Irish National Land and Industrial League was founded by Clan na Gael as a front to raise money and press political issues. Between 1879 and 1880 half a million people joined the Irish National Land League. It collected money to fund the so called Land War. It helped the tenants to resist by providing direct financial aid to evicted tenants and by paying for legal aid to carry on the struggle in the courts. In America the League publicized the anti-landlord case and gained much public sympathy and support. However, an ideological split in the League led to a division of the fund raising activities between the Irish National League and the Irish World Land League lead by Patrick Ford, editor of *The Irish World* newspaper.

After a trip to America by Parnell's sisters, Anna and Fannie Parnell, to raise funds, American women formed The Ladies Land League. In Cleveland, Ohio they defied the Anglophile Bishop Gilmour who opposed their efforts and the cause of Irish freedom.

Charles Stewart Parnell was from the landlord class. He was elected head of the Irish Parliamentary Party in 1880. He proposed a policy of obstruction in British Parliament which allowed the Irish cause to make an impact on purely British issues. He toured the United States in order to gain American political and financial support. With funding from America, Parnell's party became the most effective one in Parliament.

After noting the success of the Irish Parliamentary Party Prime Minister Gladstone sought a coalition with his Liberal Party. In 1881 Gladstone, with Parnell's support, pushed through the Land Act which guaranteed farmers a stable tenure at a fair rent. This act started the destruction of manorialism in Ireland and moved closer to peasant control of the land. Parnell, however, wanted the Land Act to include those peasants who were in arrears, so he protested. He was jailed while Ireland hovered on the brink of a massive insurrection. Gladstone proceeded to meet with Parnell in Kilmainham Jail, Dublin and agreed that if Parnell supported the Gladstone proposal an amendment would eliminate arrears and end coercion. This was called the Kilmainham Treaty. Throughout Parnell's imprisonment the Ladies Land League led by his sisters ran the movement.

From this point on Parnell switched from obstruction to a balance of power approach through cooperation with the Liberal Party. This move angered the Clan na Gael who were preparing for and ideologically committed to revolt. Home rule rather than a republic became the object of Parnell's politics. The Party with Liberal help did manage to get two home rule bills debated, one in 1880 which failed and another in 1893 which passed Commons but was vetoed by the House of Lords.

Parnell, one of Ireland's most effective leaders, was a danger to the British Tory element. The Tories played an important role in having Parnell named in a divorce action by Captain O'Shea against his wife Kitty. Kitty was Parnell's mistress and later his wife. The Catholic Church and the British Tories proceeded to ruin him, forcing the Liberals to back off in supporting him. He was replaced as head of the Irish Party but refused to accept it. He took his case to the people and traveled on a speaking tour around Ireland. However, church opposition was strong and unyielding. He was not able to regain his position or power. On October 6, 1881, at age 45 he died at his home in Avondale, a death possibly hastened by the psychosocial stress of his struggle with moralistic prejudice.

The Fall of Parnell to 1916

Justin McCarthy, who replaced Parnell, was an ineffective leader but by 1901 the United Irish League of America was founded to fund the Irish Parliamentary Party once again. It is estimated that Irish-American funds paid the allowances for half the Irish Party until 1911, and covered most of its election expenses in 1906 and 1910. The Party during this period was able to play a part in forcing the House of Commons to curb the power of the House of Lords in 1911.

The Irish Parliamentary Party moved for home rule in 1912, but the conservatives and Carsonites fought it. John Carson, a Dublin unionist, did not want partition as suggested by British liberals and only reluctantly accepted it at a later date. The Irish Party under John Redmond angered many nationalists by suggesting they would give up four Ulster counties minus the cities of Derry and Newry. Later when Redmond agreed to support the British in World War I he destroyed the United Irish League of America and with it his financial base in the United States.

In America, the Boer War in 1898 stimulated a resurgence of Irish-American nationalism. Irish-Americans denounced the war, organized mass meetings and even sent some volunteers. By 1900 the Clan na Gael had reorganized and began an attack on an alleged secret alliance with Great Britain. President McKinley offered to help settle the war between the British and the Boers fearing an alliance of anti-imperialists, Irish-Americans and German-Americans. In 1900 both American political parties had planks denouncing the Boer War. The United Irish Society also actively protested the war and sent 500 volunteers to aid the Boers.

Between 1897-1911 Irish-Americans had a great impact on Anglo-American relations. The Irish were important in the defeat of three out of four treaties during this period and in 1905 Secretary of State Hay admitted the influence of Clan na Gael in opposition to treaties in 1897 and 1904. The Clan na Gael also began to publicize the Indian nationalist cause by 1906. An Irish-American/German-American alliance prevented the United States from supporting Britain in its attempts to limit German and Russian expansion in the Far East.

The 1916 Easter Rising to the Civil War

The Clan na Gael wanted the United States to remain neutral during World War I. The Ancient Order of Hibernians (AOH), however, entered into a formal agreement with the German-American alliance and supported the Germans. The British government had to work actively and extensively to combat Irish-American opposition to the war. They encouraged pro-British elements in the United States government and media to carry out an active campaign against hyphenated Americans. President Wilson was particularly upset by Irish-American behavior which he considered disloyal and it may have influenced his attitudes toward the Irish question after the war.

The Clan na Gael was the only Irish-American organization to know about the 1916 Rising before it occurred and they provided some of the funds. Roger Casement was given $10,000 in Clan money to purchase weapons from Germany. The Easter Rising stunned the world as the rebels held Dublin for a week, but it was the British brutal repression of the Rising that turned many Irish and American people toward the cause of the rebels. The public execution of the leaders was a crucial political and sociopsychological mistake by the British. Britain actually began to fear that the United States might break the blockade of the Central Powers.

When the United States entered the war in 1917, Irish-Americans had to prove their loyalty. They rallied to the call and fought bravely against the Central Powers. Regiments like the largely Irish Fighting 69th became almost legendary. Joyce Kilmer, the promising American poet attached to the 69th, enshrined some of their deeds in poetry before his battlefield death. Irish groups, though, soon mobilized themselves to have Ireland included in the peace talks.

In Ireland Sinn Fein achieved a massive political victory in the British parliamentary elections of 1918. The anti-union forces won 73 seats but refused to sit in Parliament and set up the first Dail in Dublin in January of 1919. The elections showed that nationalists were a majority in all but 2-1/2 counties out of Ireland's 32. The British refused to recognize the nationalist mandate and commenced the Anglo-Irish war against the government set up by the Dail. The Irish Republican Army (IRA) was recognized as the defender of the

Irish Republic. The British and the IRA fought a long brutal guerilla war, from 1918 to 1921, in which the IRA received much support from America.

When World War I was over Irish-Americans pressed for self-determination in Ireland. The Friends of Irish Freedom (FOIF), founded in March 1910 by the Clan na Gael, became a leading proponent of Irish self determination. The Friends of Irish Freedom elected three Irish-American representatives to the Peace Conference at Versailles. This was done at an Irish Race convention in Philadelphia during February 1919. However, the Irish-American representatives were refused admission to the Versailles talks. Further, the British prevented Irish representatives such as Eamon DeValera from attending the conference.

The Irish-American reaction was to step up pressure on the American Congress. On March 4, 1919, the House and Senate supported the idea of Irish representation at the Peace Conference by votes of 216 to 45 and 60 to 1 respectively.

President Wilson, however, disliked the Irish-American interference. He thought they were disloyal hyphenated Americans. Wilson was also an anti-Catholic bigot which may have been related to his Ulster protestant roots or more probably to his Anglophilic attitude toward British culture and institutions. Furthermore, he detested Judge Daniel Cohalan, one of the Irish-American leaders. Even without the influence of the above factors Wilson obviously needed Britain's help to form the League of Nations. The League was Wilson's dream, thus he would never have risked alienating Britain over Ireland. Wilson said that self-determination only applied to the lands of the former Central Powers, not to those of allies like Britain.

The Irish Race Convention representatives traveled to Ireland to support DeValera and encourage rebellion. At home the Clan na Gael and its front, the Friends of Irish Freedom (FOIF), launched a campaign against Wilson's cherished dream, the League of Nations. Led by Judge Cohalan they held large mass meetings and took out full page newspaper ads against the League wherever Wilson traveled to promote it. They collaborated with former WASP opponents such as senators Borah and Lodge, who were isolationists, in order to defeat it. Wilson died knowing that America never ratified the League which was the lynch pin of his view of world co-operation.

DeValera arrived in America in 1919 during the Anglo-Irish War in order to raise funds and gather more support for the struggle against Britain.   He sold bond certificates redeemable after independence. It is estimated that the American Commission on Conditions in Ireland and the American Commission for Relief in Ireland collected over $5,000,000. DeValera did split with Judge Cohalan because his group was spending some Irish Victory Fund moneys ($100,000) to fight entry into the League rather than sending it to Ireland. In 1920 DeValera created the American Association for the Recognition of the Irish Republic which meant that all funds went to the struggle in Ireland.

In the Anglo-Irish War the IRA fought the British to a standstill and actually controlled most of the countryside, even to the extent of setting up courts and other institutions outside the British system. The death of the Lord Mayor of Cork, Terence MacSwiney, in Brixton Prison after a 75 day hunger strike had a significant influence on American as well as world opinion on the nature of the struggle in Ireland. MacSwiney's heroic death exerted great pressure on Prime Minister Lloyd George to affect a settlement.

However, the settlement came in the form of partition. The treaty ending the war in 1921 and creating the 26-county Irish Free State was not acceptable to radical republicans. Most Irish-Americans accepted the treaty as the best deal, possibly partly because they never did understand the politics of home rule dominion status or the nature of Irish nationalist goals in Ireland.

The modern world's first revolution against a major colonial power was aborted and at least temporarily lost by partition. Britain's retention of six out of the nine original counties of historic Ulster was a massive gerrymander. A gerrymander that assured a loyalist majority and allowed a majority in one small area to dictate the fate of the entire island in which they were a minority. It laid the historic foundations for the present war in northern Ireland.

The anti-treaty forces in Ireland refused to accept the settlement that left Ireland divided. A civil war broke out between the pro-treaty and anti-treaty forces. Families were split and brother fought against brother. The "Free State" forces, supported by the British with weapons and money, brutally repressed the anti-treaty forces. In fact, the "Free State" executed more Irish nationalists than the British did during the period 1916-1921. The "Free State" forces eventually won and the anti-treaty forces led by DeValera went underground. The strife created splits in Irish society that continue to the present day.

Most Irish-Americans were confused by the civil war as Irish Republicans fought over an ideal that most Americans did not understand. The brutality of the conflict disgusted them and in general turned their attention away from Ireland. From the Irish Civil War to the beginning of the northern Ireland civil rights movement most Irish-Americans considered partition the best that could be hoped for. Of course the more knowledgeable and ideologically aware Irish-Americans understood the republican position and continued to support the struggle to unite Ireland.

However, between 1916 and 1931 it is estimated that 800,000 or more joined Irish-American national organizations that were working toward Irish freedom. The largely working class membership of these organizations contributed over $10,000,000 to the Sinn Fein/IRA struggle against Britain.

From Civil War to Civil Rights

With partial independence for the Irish Free State the vast majority of Irish-Americans thought that the issue was settled as best as it could be. As immigration from Ireland decreased after independence, American interest waned. However, small groups led by Joe McGarrity of the Clan na Gael continued to support the various campaigns to free the six partitioned counties.

For the most part occasional attempts in the United States to rally mass support against partition went nowhere. When Ireland remained neutral in World War II most Irish-Americans were shocked. Irish-Americans, who tend to be a patriotic lot, felt let down by DeValera and the land of their ancestors. They had no conception of Irish fears that Britain would use the war to reassert its influence as well as its presence in Ireland. People who fought 800 years to rid themselves of invaders had no intention of allowing them to reoccupy their land no matter what the pretense. IRA campaigns in the 1930's, 1940's and mid-1950's received little attention in the American press. Most Irish-Americans were totally uninformed about what was going on in the six counties.

Civil Rights to War

In the 1960's the Civil Rights Movement in the six counties began as a non-violent protest modeled on that of Dr. Martin Luther King Jr. in the United States. The movement was a non-sectarian one that proposed local civil reforms within the United Kingdom. Most Americans became aware of this movement in Ireland for the first time when TV showed the violence associated with a long march from Belfast to Derry. On the six o'clock news the Irish question bolted into the spotlight as Americans saw civil rights marchers beaten by loyalist reactionaries with the active and passive assistance of the Royal Ulster Constabulary (RUC).

Scenes of loyalist attacks on nationalist ghettos in an attempt to burn them out appeared on prime time American news. Likewise nationalist counter attacks which led to the barricading of their ghettos and the appearance of regular British Army patrols on the streets of northern Ireland raced across TV screens. For many Americans who were ignorant of the history of the six counties, the soldiers seemed to be welcome peacekeepers. But on January 20, 1972, the United States media presented the story of Bloody Sunday as British paratroopers shot and killed 14 unarmed civil rights marchers on the streets of Derry. In Dublin an angry mob burned the British embassy to the ground. Americans along with the rest of the world protested the army's brutality.

The bloody suppression of the northern Ireland Civil Rights Movement in the late 60's and early 70's reawakened Irish-American interest in partition. Bloody Sunday may be considered a watershed event in contemporary Irish history. The fall of the Civil Rights struggle was accompanied by renewed calls for complete British withdrawal.

What started as a reform movement had now evolved into a war of liberation. The Irish-American community, however, found itself largely unprepared and in disarray. The once powerful Irish American National organizations like the Ancient Order of Hibernians (AOH) and the Clan na Gael were only a shadow of their past. In many instances the memberships were declining and increasingly aged. The Irish-born population in the United States, long a bulwark of Irish-American Nationalism, numbered only 190,000 in 1970. The Catholic Church was moving into ecumenical rapprochement with Protestants and did not wish to raise the sectarianism, real or imagined.

Liberals, the champions of human rights around the world, were worried about being associated with violence. Although initially moved by the vicious attacks of loyalists on the civil rights marches and the pogroms in nationalist ghettos, most liberals disassociated themselves from the issue when the nationalists hit back at their oppressors. Further, liberal America seems to shy away from Ireland because of allegations of Catholic versus Protestant sectarianism. A strong undercurrent of anti-Catholicism runs through American society, and as Schlesinger has suggested anti-Catholicism is liberal America's last socially acceptable prejudice. One is moved to ponder how much this ideological stance affects the attitude of America toward the struggle in northern Ireland, especially the media and liberal political leaders. Affluent Irish-Americans many generations removed from their Irish roots, especially the sentimental St. Patrick's Day variety, were embarrassed by the violence and revolutionary rhetoric. They were more worried about what their neighbors or fellow workers would think rather than about social justice for the suffering nationalist minority in Ireland.

This, then, was the situation faced by Irish-American activists who were attempting to revive the old political network on behalf of the beleaguered nationalists of the northeast. One of the earliest organizations that appeared was the National Association for Irish Justice (NAIJ) founded in 1968 to support the northern Ireland Civil Rights Association (NICRA) in Ireland. In 1969 Bernadette Devlin of NICRA, and the youngest person ever elected to the British Parliament came to the United States on a speaking tour to raise funds for the northeast. She raised an estimated $200,000 but she could have raised more if her political ideals had not clashed with powerful Irish-American leaders like Mayor Richard Daley of Chicago. Bernadette refused to back away from her support for Black power advocates, such as the Black Panthers, and this upset a number of powerful potential supporters. In March of 1970 Bernadette gave her key to New York City to the Black Panthers. Bernadette was an impressive spokesperson - bright, articulate and full of fire. She became disgusted with the political naivete and overt racism of many Irish-Americans. Bernadette returned to Ireland with less money than many had hoped but with her ideals and social conscience intact. In 1970 the NAIJ split up as a result of ideological conflicts over the direction of the American phase of the struggle. The three factions that split off were supporters of the Provisional IRA, the Official IRA and some Trotskyites.

The NAIJ was reorganized as the National Association for Irish Freedom (NAIF) but split again in May of 1972 into the Irish Rebel Theater, An Claidheamh Soluis, and the Coalition Committee for Ulster Justice. The highpoints of the NAIF early history involved protest activity surrounding the jailing of the Ft. Worth Five and a St. Patrick's Day Parade protest against the Bloody Sunday massacre in Derry.

Of the groups that evolved from the early Irish-American civil rights coalition, Noraid founded in 1970 was to become the heart and soul of fund raising and political education with respect to the northeast. The Irish northern Aid Committee (Noraid) gathered its early strength in the old Irish strongholds of New York, Philadelphia, Boston, Chicago and San Francisco, but the movement spread quickly to other Irish communities across the United States, from Detroit to Butte, Montana.

Noraid found its supporters in a variety of places but the backbone consisted of Irish people with strong northern ties. Irish and Irish-American people with a strong family tradition of republicanism were also prominent. Civil libertarians who objected to the abuse of human rights by the British, as well as ordinary people simply responding to the violence and suffering, often joined the cause. Finally, a number of younger radicals who recognized parallels with colonial and neocolonial struggle around the world were drawn to the struggle in Ireland as well. Interestingly, liberal groups such as the National Conference of Christians and Jews were silent, especially when one considers their outspoken stance on the problems of Russian Jews. Historically the Irish-American press has always played an important part in the nationalist struggle, but the existent press was weak and, for the most part, gossip-oriented at this time. This situation was a far cry from the heyday of *The Gaelic American, The Citizen* and *The Irish World*. However, in 1970 *The*

Irish People was founded to bring news of the struggle in Ireland to the American people. It also carried news of movement activities in the United States, letters to the editor and examples of political reaction and commentary by American politicians, journalists and other people of influence. After a rough start and much harassment by the U.S. government, by 1972 the paper was on solid footing. Today it has developed into a solid political weekly presenting an alternative view of the war in Ireland.

Noraid is the organization that most concerns the British, Irish and American governments. Noraid has been charged with raising money for guns by each of those governments as well as much of the news media in those countries. However, over ten years of monitoring the books and the activities of Noraid by all three governments has not produced any evidence of misuse of the funds collected for humanitarian purposes. In northern Ireland interviews with solicitors, politicians and ordinary people in nationalist areas seem to affirm that the money does go for humanitarian purposes. The families of republican political prisoners have depended on weekly Noraid money to supplement their dole funds and locally-raised funds in their effort to survive the deprived conditions that characterize occupied Ireland.

The purpose of the false charges by the governments involved appears to be related to setting a political tone or climate which excuses harassment of activists. It is also an attempt to scare less committed people from contributing funds, although I believe they misread the American working class attitude toward where their money goes. My interviews and observations indicate that working class - especially blue collar - Americans wouldn't care if their money went for guns. In fact I have found that many would give even more money if they knew it went for guns.

Until recently lobbying efforts at the executive and legislative levels have not been too productive. But efforts to enlist the support of individual congressmen have been quite successful. The Ad Hoc Committee on Irish Affairs in Congress headed initially by Mario Biaggi is the largest ad hoc committee in the history of Congress and has an average of well over 100 members per session and is bipartisan as well as multi-ethnic in nature. It has been maintained in recent years by Congresspersons such as Tom Manton, Ben Gilman, Hamilton Fish and Peter King.

Attempts to enlist media support have been difficult. The media are generally poorly informed, uninterested and/or hostile. The pro-British bias of the national media is a major stumbling block toward developing a broader consciousness among the American people. With the possible exceptions of the early days of the civil rights movement and the more recent hunger strikes, media coverage has been shallow and misinformed. The media has been too heavily dependent on British government releases rather than independent investigative reporting. Given the most recent research by Curtis (1984) on British government management of media information on Ireland in England, it is not surprising that American media is so deficient.

A number of Irish-American activists have been arrested and charged by the United States government, and some such as the Ft. Worth Five served unconscionable prison sentences during the Nixon years. Others such as Michael Flannery and his codefendants were acquitted by a jury trial of all charges including gun running. Irish-Americans have engineered successful court battles to prevent extradition of Irish political prisoners to Britain. In fact they had been so successful that the State Department and the Thatcher government pushed a supplemental extradition treaty through the Senate in order to circumvent the judicial process and shift the decision on political status to State Department bureaucrats. Irish-American groups mustered heavy opposition to ratification and delayed ratification of the treaty. However, after Britain allowed the United States to use British bases to bomb Libya, the treaty was approved as a gift to Thatcher.

A number of Irish-American groups have emerged to play an active role in the American phase of the struggle in northern Ireland. These groups include Irish Northern Aid, the Irish National Caucus, the Ancient Order of Hibernians, the Irish-American Fenian Society, the National Political Education Committee (NPEC), the Irish-American Unity Conference, the Irish-American Defense Fund, and the Clan na Gael as well as a variety of local groups without national affiliation. The organizations provide a variety of functions which can be grouped into the following broad categories:

1.   Public education on the issue and its historical background,
2.   The organization of public demonstrations of support and
        letter writing campaigns to local or national media,
3.   Direct and indirect lobbying with American politicians,
4.   Humanitarian aid for the families and dependents of
        Irishpolitical prisoners,
5.   The organization of Irish-American prisoners defense funds
        to aid those who run afoul of the United States government.

These organizations vary in their level of involvement and some are
not involved in all aspects of the support network.

In characterizing the active participants one might begin by
making it clear what they are not. The average activist is not a
sloppy, sentimental St. Patrick's Day Irishman that loves the blarney
stone, leprechauns and Danny Boy. They are not zaney, romantic
sectarian bogtrotters, nor are they narrow-minded racist
Anglophobes. These types of characterization are the product largely
of the Irish and British governments and appear to be defensive
rationalizations for public consumption. Unfounded ridicule and
character assassination like racism are simplistic ways to discredit
individuals or groups that disagree with orthodox belief.

In contrast to the above characterizations most of the actively
involved people, especially the leadership, are well-informed and
dedicated, with some direct experience in the north. They are not
put off by the necessary violence which characterizes the struggle in
the occupied Ireland. They are a hard nosed, combative group that
believe in the cause for which they work. Further, they are people
who are confident with their own place in American society which
they feel has been earned by years of sacrifice and loyalty to the
United States and its institutions. A great number are also cognizant
of the parallels between northern Ireland and other trouble spots
around the world.

Recently a combination of Irish-American activists, powerful
Irish-American business people and American politicians have
convinced the Clinton Administration to take a more positive stand
on the situation in northern Ireland in an effort to pressure a
peaceful solution acceptable to all parties. In early 1994 an important
step in a new direction was taken when the Clinton Administration
allowed Gerry Adams, the president of Sinn Fein, to enter the US to

present the republican point of view. At the same time many of the same groups and persons have lobbied with the Irish Nationalist political parties in the six counties to affect a ceasefire by the IRA so that Britain will no longer be able to avoid talking to all shades of Irish Nationalist political opinion.

Theoretical Explanations

Various theories have been proposed to explain the longevity of Irish-American involvement in Irish Freedom struggles. Brown (1966) in a much-quoted study of Irish-American nationalism suggests that participation was part of a process of the quasiexorcism of the Irish-American psyche. According to Brown the intensity of the nativistic opposition to the Irish immigrants convinced the Irish-Americans that their acceptance required a vindication of their degraded heritage. Ireland had to be freed to gain respect for Irish-America.

Brown seems to downplay the fact that much of the nativistic opposition to the Irish-American immigrants was due to the brash outspoken Irishness of the Catholic famine immigrants. These immigrants wore their allegiance to foreign religion on their sleeve. They also exploited their experience in democratic politics in Ireland to consolidate and establish a political powerbase here in the U.S. If the Irish were really overly concerned with gaining acceptance and respect from WASP nativists and other exploiters of immigrants, why did they not give up their Catholic faith en masse? Why didn't they ally themselves with reformist WASP's rather than pragmatic machine Democrats?

Miller (1984) has claimed that homesickness cultivated an unrealistic attachment to the old country and strong perceptions of involuntary exile. It would seem that the culture shock of the new land and the realities of their early experiences in the immigrant ghettos encouraged a sentimental defense by exaggerating what was lost by immigration.   The new arrivals also offered further encouragement for other emigrants to leave the old country, and in many cases sent money home to cover emigration expenses. Miller, however, seems to downplay the reality of the trauma of the Irish diaspora. The development of the American wake that treated emigration in much the same way as actual death emphasized the tragedy and finality of emigration for a family-oriented people such as the Irish. It was the deliberate underdevelopment and political oppression of Ireland that forced directly or indirectly most of the emigration from Ireland.

Foner (1978) has called for a re-evaluation of the whole field of Irish-American working class radicalism. He perceives Irish-American nationalism as an expression of working class radicalism and cites its intimate connections with the American labor movement through such people as T.V. Powderly. Yet contrary to most historical scholarship the Irish were leaders in the most radical of the early labor movements such as Western Federation of Miners, Workingman's Benevolent Association (WBA), and Industrial Workers of the World (IWW). However, nationalist participation was not monolithic. Irish-Americans from the working class and the middle class as well as some "lace curtain" Irish took part. The composition of the movement varied locally and during different phases of the struggle. For example, the "lace curtain" Irish were able to support the Land League phase of the struggle but were scared off when the physical force tradition came to the forefront.

Simplistic, single factor theories are deficient because the origin and development of Irish-American nationalism is multi-causal. Motivating factors as well as the nature of the participants varied from one time period to the next. A sociohistorical theory that incorporates aspects of all the previous theories plus additional factors is necessary. Historically nationalism in Ireland prior to emigration, except in some specialized groups such as the United Irishmen and the Young Irelanders, was not very well developed. The nature of the lifeways of the Irish masses is instructive in this respect. The political geography of Ireland did not stress the nation as a political entity but encouraged sociopolitical identification with the townland, parish, county and occasionally the province. A great number of Irish peasants exhibited loyalty to their landlords. This situation could be expected given their lack of political rights and the constant fear that the landlord could raise the rent or evict them. To the struggling Irish peasant or landless laborers the desire for individual ownership of land overshadowed any idealism related to national integrity. In spite of this, however, every generation spawned agrarian protest of a violent nature which hint of a later organized guerilla resistance that has been associated with the Irish.

Institutionally the Catholic Church in Ireland opposed the nationalistic movement because the hierarchy feared the growing secularism and anti-clericalism associated with radical revolutionary movements on the continent. The Catholic hierarchy especially would not tolerate changes in the status quo although individual priests often encouraged revolution. Irish political leaders varied from Daniel O'Connell, who could not see the value of nationalism and preferred home rule to independence, to the Young Irelanders, who promoted cultural nationalism as a prelude to independence. O'Connell was a constitutionalist and because of his successful agitation for Catholic emancipation had the support of the masses. The Young Irelanders were revolutionary separatists who did not reject the use of violence in the quest for freedom, but when the opportunity arose they were in general too middle class to use it. The Young Irelanders did not reach enough people but did provide the ideological basis for later nationalist causes. However, the physical force tradition existed during all periods and was eventually successful in winning partial independence for the island.

In America, however, a great number of these same Irish people seemed to become ardent nationalists. Patrick Ford, editor of the influential *The Irish World*, suggested that America led the Irish peasant from the "littleness of countyism into the broad feeling of nationalism." Ford's observation is probably correct and such a shift of focus was most likely due to a variety of factors among which were:

1.   The common ghetto experience and its institutions,regardless of their local Irish origins, forced the Irish to assume a larger identity.
2.   A common historical heritage of colonial exploitation cultivated a broad hatred of England which characterized most Irish emigrants.
3.   The Anglo-American nativists hated the Irish and their church and thus encouraged solidarity.
4.   The observations in America that poverty need not be permanent made the immigrant realize that the poverty at home was not their fault but was imposed by an outside foreign force, namely England.

5.   A literature of cultural nationalism, largely developed by the
       ex-Young Irelanders, made the immigrants feel proud to be
       Irish by developing a Celtic mythology to counter WASP
       superiority and by providing them with information to
       combat anti-Irish critics.

6.   The influence of the Irish American press such as *The Irish
       World, The Citizen, The Nation,* and *The Gaelic American*
       that championed the cause of the Irish masses and taught
       Irish nationalism along with adaptation to life in America.

7.   The improving economic situation and a feeling of self worth
       for some afforded the opportunity to involve oneself in the
       struggles at home rather than the necessity of total
       commitment to the everyday struggle to survive.

8.   The increasing involvement of Irish-Americans in the
       radicalism of the Labor Movement that forced many
       Irish-Americans to view the struggle in Ireland as part of a
       worldwide struggle against inequality and colonialism.

9.   There has been increasing involvement of many Irish-
       Americans from the New Deal Era to the present in the
       area of radical politics and public advocacy. This
       involvement forced the participants to consider the situation
       in northern Ireland as a colonial survival from the 19th
       century and not deserving of democratic support.

10.   Since the 1970's the reawakening of ethnicity among many
       Irish-Americans has led to a re-examination of their roots.
       A greater knowledge of the oppressive history of Ireland has
       led a number of individuals to take an active role in the
       present day struggle.

CHAPTER 1

GENERAL REFERENCES

1   Akenson, D.A. 1973. *The United States and Ireland.* Harvard University. Cambridge, MA.

A well organized, articulate discussion of Irish Nationalist issues in relation to the United States up to and including the destruction of the civil rights movement in the early 1970's. A generally fair discussion of the history of Ireland and its partition with the exception of a pro-British bias when discussing the role of the IRA in the 1970's.

2   Bagenal, H. 1882. *The American Irish and Their Influence on Irish Politics.* K. Paul, Trench, Co., London. (Reprinted, 1971, Ozer, New York)

An early work by a not so sympathetic author that first chronicles the history of Irish immigration to America. The second half of the book deals with the role of Irish-Americans in the efforts of Irish Revolutionaries to remove Britain from Ireland. The author seems quite taken with the influence of the Young Ireland Movement of the 1840's on the Irish masses during the Land War. He seems to be appalled at the audaciousness of the Irish Revolutionaries. The author was an English traveler in America.

3   Brown, Thomas N. 1953. Nationalism and the Irish Peasant, 1800-1848. *Review of Politics*, 15:4:403-445.

A study of the development of Irish nationalism among Irish peasants from the rising of 1798 to the Young Ireland Movement of the Famine years. Especially good on the interaction of sociopolitical factors and socioeconomic conditions that affected the genesis of Irish nationalism. An important background study for those seeking to study the Irish-American aspect of Irish nationalism.

4   ____. 1955. *Irish-American Nationalism, 1848-1891.* Harvard University. PhD. Dissertation.

An historical study of the origins and development of Irish-American nationalism from the days of the Young Ireland Movement to the Gaelic cultural revival in the late nineteenth century. It is a more developed work than his celebrated book which tended to both simplify and modify what appears in this original work.

5   ____. 1956. The Origins and Character of Irish-American Nationalism. *Review of Politics,* 18:3:327-358.

An article that is a spin off from Brown's PhD dissertation noted above. It traces the development of Irish nationalism in America while promoting Brown's thesis that Irish-American nationalism was directed toward American not Irish ends, that is the vindication of the degraded Irish immigrant in America.

6   ____. 1966. *Irish-American Nationalism 1870-1890.* J.B. Lippincott, New York.

A much cited study of the origins and development of Irish-American nationalism. Brown suggests that participation in Irish-American nationalism was a result of an immigrant quest to be accepted in America. Intense nationwide opposition to the Irish was seen as related to their degraded heritage thus Ireland had to be freed to gain respect for Irish-Americans. An interesting but simplistic view. This study is a must for anyone studying Irish-American nationalism. However, his original dissertation (1955) is more complete in its discussion of the issues.

7   Calkin, Homer L. 1954. The United States Government and the Irish. *Irish Historical Studies,* 9:28-52.

A valuable article that identifies sources of research

materials in the United States National Archives on the political significance of the Irish-Americans in Anglo-Irish relations along with other topics like immigration and naturalization and economic social conditions of Irish-Americans. A valuable bibliographic source.

8   Collins, P.A. 1901-03. Ireland's Dream of Nationality. In: *Modern Eloquence*. T.B. Reed et al, eds. J.D. Morris, Philadelphia. Pp. 257-60.
        A brief statement on the nationalism of Irish-American leader Patrick Collins.

9   Duff, John B. 1971. Allegiance to Two Flags. In: *The Irish in the United States*. J.B. Duff. Wadsworth Publishing Co., Belmont, CA. Pp. 65-72.
        A brief chapter in a more general book on Irish-American history that deals with Irish-American involvement in Ireland from the Fenians to the Irish Civil War. Well done.

10   Farrell, M. 1985. *Sheltering the Fugitive? The Extradition of Irish Offenders*. Mercier Press, Cork.
        A brief work on the extradition of Irish political offenders, which makes reference to political refuge and the United States Constitution.

11   Flannery, John B. 1982. *Rights Bought in Blood: Abandoned in Apathy*. Address to the AOH Convention. San Antonio TX.
        A pamphlet that documents the history of the Irish-American contribution to the growth and development of American independence and its relationship to the present day rights of Irish-Americans to speak out on the situation in the 6 counties today.

12   Fleming, Thomas. 1979. The Green Flag in America. *American Heritage*, 30:4:50-63.
        A brief popular history of Irish-American

involvement with Irish nationalism from Daniel O'Connell to the Irish Civil War. An interesting synthesis of groups and personalities related to the struggle. It is somewhat marred by a naive attempt to relate to the present struggle in northeast Ireland by commenting on the hands-off attitude of some of today's Irish-American elites such as Kennedy, Carey, Moynihan and O'Neill.

13   Foner, Eric. 1978. Class, Ethnicity and Radicalism in the Gilded Age: The Land League and Irish America. *Marxist Perspectives*, 2:6-55.

An excellent study that perceives Irish-American nationalism as an expression of working class radicalism, especially in relation to its connections with the labor movement. Foner calls for a reevaluation of the whole field of Irish-American working class radicalism which has been ignored or downplayed by most historians. An excellent source of material on the Irish Land League, Clan na Gael and the relationship of the labor movement to Irish-American nationalism.

14   Funchion, Michael F. ed. 1983. *Irish American Voluntary Organizations*. Greenwood, Westport, Conn.

A marvelous compendium of short annotations and longer essays on the various Irish-American organizations in America. It includes many articles and reference to all the Irish-American nationalist organizations. An obligatory reference for those in Irish-American Studies.

15   Greeley, A.M. 1986. The Nationalist Cause. In: *The Irish-Americans: Rise to Money and Power*. A.M. Greeley. Harper and Row, New York. pp. 90-105.

A chapter in Greeley's most recent work on Irish-America, that attempts to place the present role of the Irish-American Nationalist in historical perspective. However it is sketchy and exceptionally naive on the situation related to the 6 counties today.

16   Hachey, Thomas E. 1984. Irish Republicanism Yesterday
          and the Dilemma of Irish Americans. In: *Ethnicity and
          War*. W.A. VanHorn and T.V. Tonnesone, eds. University
          of Wisconsin System American Ethnic Studies Co-ordinating
          Committee. Milwaukee, pp. 150-173.

                    A survey of Irish republicanism in America from
          John   O'Mahoney and Michael Doheny in 1858 until the
          present day. The historical coverage up to the 1960's is
          standard. However from the 1970's on Hachey's work is a
          massive diatribe against the IRA and its supporters,
          complete with statements that are undocumentable such as
          one of the major conduits for smuggling arms from the US
          to northern Ireland in recent times has been Noraid. He is
          also very selective in his interpretation of such issues as
          British power sharing proposals, and Congressional and
          political support in the United States for the Irish struggle.

17   Hachey, T., J.M. Hernon Jr. and L.J. McCaffrey. 1989.
          Irish America and the Contemporary Conflict in Northern
          Ireland. In: *The Irish Experience*. Hachey, T. et al.,
          Prentice Hall, Englewood Cliffs, New Jersey. Pp. 248-259.

                    A naive elitist view of Irish America and the present
          conflict in the northeast of Ireland by 3 highly esteemed
          historians who never really investigated the topic at the
          grassroots. It is full of overgeneralizations and errors.

18   Ibson, J.D. Two Flags: The Meaning of Irish American
          Nationalism. In: *Will The World Break Your Heart?* J.D.
          Ibson. Garland, New York. Pp. 62-95.

                    An interesting chapter in a larger work on Irish-
          American identity, that highlights four Irish-American
          Nationalists, John Boyle O'Reilly, Joseph Ignatius Clarke,
          John Quinn and Bourke Cockran. His discussion of Irish-
          American dual allegiance centers around these four
          individuals. The author concludes that Thomas Brown's
          thesis of Irish-American nationalism as a proving ground for
          assimilation is too simplistic since he feels that assimilation
          was not viewed as desirable and in actuality was not realized.

19   Joyce, W.L. 1976. Immigrant Nationalism in the Irish-American Press. In: *Editors and Ethnicity.* W.L. Joyce. Arno Press New York. Pp. 74-100.
        A chapter from a PhD dissertation on *Editors and Ethnicity.* It deals with the role of the Irish-American press in promoting an awareness of Ireland, its culture and political situation during the 19th century.

20   Kiernan, J.L. 1964. *Ireland and America Versus England.* George W. Pattison, Detroit.
        A book by an Irish-American, Brigadier General Kieran, that depicts the struggle in Ireland and America as a fight between democracy and the rights of man versus aristocracy and the rights of kings.

21   McCaffrey, L.J. 1973. Irish Nationalism and Irish Catholicism: A Study in Cultural Identity. *Church History,* 42:4:1-11.
        McCaffrey's study of the close relationship between Irish nationalism and catholicism is clouded by his blind acceptance of West British or Tory revisionist interpretation of Irish history. It is also greatly affected by his lack of up to date, first hand knowledge of the situation in northeastern Ireland as well as his own long time bias toward constitutional nationalism rather than physical force or revolutionary nationalism.

22   _____. 1976. Irish America and the Course of Irish Nationalism. In: *The Irish Diaspora in America.* L.J. McCaffrey. Indiana U., Bloomington. pp. 107-137.
        A chapter in a much respected work on Irish-American history. Historically accurate and objective until the author has to deal with the situation in the 6 counties today. This portion is clouded by naive, emotional posturing apparently influenced by both Irish Tory revisionism and media mythology.

23   ____. 1976. *Irish Nationalism and the American Contribution*. Arno Press, New York.

A fine collection of 5 essays on American contributions to Irish nationalism including classic articles by Thomas N. Brown, Alan Ward and Larry McCaffrey.

24   McGarrity, J. 1942. *Celtic Moods and Memories*. Devin-Adair, New York.

The reminiscence of Joe McGarrity idealist, dreamer, poet and Irish-American revolutionary who spent a lifetime and 2 fortunes in the struggle for Irish freedom including the post partition era's anti-treaty republicanism.

25   Miller, K. 1980. *Emigrants and Exiles: Irish Culture and Irish Emigration to North America*. 1790-1922. Irish Historical Studies, 22:36:1-29.

A lengthy well written cultural\historical analysis of Irish emigration from 1790 to 1922. It includes a great deal of material on the origins and role of Irish nationalism among Irish immigrants to America. It presents arguments for Miller thesis that Irish-American nationalism had its roots in distorted, alienated interpretation of themselves as involuntary exiles coupled with an inordinate sense of homesickness. However, Miller seems to ignore the fact that in reality the deliberate underdevelopment and political oppression of Ireland forced directly or indirectly most of the emigration from Ireland.

26   Miller, K.A. 1985. *Emigrants and Exiles: Ireland and the Irish Exodus to North America*. Oxford University Press, New York.

The major work on Irish emigration to North America, a very scholarly, detailed analysis of the process of emigration. It contains many references to Irish-American involvement in Irish Nationalist activities. Even if you don't agree with all of Miller's interpretations this work is an invaluable resource for those in Irish studies.

27   Moody, T.W. 1967. Irish-American Nationalism. *Irish Historical Studies*, 15:60:438-445.
        A detailed analytical review essay of T.N. Browns' book *Irish-American Nationalism 1870-1890*, an excellent piece.

28   Murphy, J.H. 1980. The Influence of America on Irish Nationalism. In: *America and Ireland 1776-1976*. D.N. Doyle and O.D. Edwards, eds. Greenwood Press, Westport, Conn. Pp. 105-116.
        A brief summary of the historical contributions of the Irish in America to the development of Irish nationalism by a scholar unsympathetic to republicanism. He therefore takes some unobjective closing shots at Irish-American involvement in the struggle today.

29   Murray, S. 1934. *Ireland's Fight for Freedom and the Irish*. U.S.A. Workers Library Publishers, New York. 15p.
        A brief pamphlet by Sean Murray of the Irish Workers Clubs of the United States on the relationship of the Irish in the USA to the struggle for Irish Freedom. It is a radical analysis of the oppression of Irish and Irish-American workers and the need for a class struggle in both countries.

30   Rice, C.E. 1985. *Divided Ireland: A Cause for American Concern*. Tyholland Press, Notre Dame, IN.
        A brief introduction to the situation in northeast Ireland by a noted law professor from the University of Notre Dame. It attempts to explain the reasons why Americans should take an active interest in promoting peace and social justice in the 6 counties.

31   Rodechko, James P. 1967. *Patrick Ford and His Search for America*. University of Connecticut. Ph.D. Dissertation. (reprinted in 1976 by Arno Press)
        A study of a noted Irish-American journalist and publisher of *The Irish World*. It contains much material on

Ford's Irish republicanism and the efforts his paper made in the cause of Irish struggle against landlordism and British occupation.

32   Wibberly, L.P. 1958. Ireland Shall Be Free. In: *The Coming of the Green*. L.P. Wibberly. Henry Holt, New York. pp. 161-170.
       A brief chapter in a popular work on Irish immigration that addresses Irish-American attitudes toward the Irish struggle in the late 19th and early 20th centuries.

33   Wittke, C. 1956. Anglophobia and Irish Nationalism. In: *The Irish in America*. C. Wittke. Russell and Russell, New York. pp. 161-171.
       A chapter in a classic book length account of the Irish in America. An interesting historical account of Irish-American involvement in the culture and politics of Irish nationalism especially in the late 1800's. Other chapters in the book contain a great amount of material on other periods of Irish Nationalist history.

CHAPTER 2

THE RISE OF IRISH NATIONALISM FROM THE
UNITED IRISHMEN THROUGH THE FENIANS

34   Anon.   1871.   Fenianism By One Who Knows.
Contemporary Review, 19:301-316.
Discusses the development of the Fenian movement
and the Fenian Brotherhood and how it gained popularity
and power in the United States and Ireland.   A brief
chronological account of major Fenian meetings and
conventions as well as the development of the political split
in the American Fenians is included. The best short account
dealing with the early years of the Fenian movement in the
United States.

35   Anon. 1868. Fenianism in America. *Bentleys Miscellaney*,
63:129-133.
A short article that attempts to show the Irish in
America in a unfavorable light. It alleges that the Irish
supported slavery and hated the African-Americans.

36   Anon. 1868. Fenianism - Why Is It? *Putnam's Monthly
Magazine*. May, 1868. Pp. 543-48.
Deals with how the execution of the Manchester
martyrs revitalized Fenianism in the US.

37   Anon.   1867.   Transatlantic Fenianism.   *Blackwoods
Magazine*, May 1867. Pp 590-606.
An anti-Fenian piece that stresses anti-Irish
stereotypes of belligerency and drunkenness. It makes no
attempt at an analysis of the movement.

38   Bell, J.B. 1990. The Transcendental Irish Republic: The
          Dream of Diaspora. *Journal of Political Science,* 18:148-168.
                  A discussion of the ideology of Irish seperatism and
          its American connections since the mid-19th century. It is
          written in Bell's factual but cynical style. It is also
          dominated by his disinclination to put heavy blame on
          Britain.

39   Bew, P. 1979. *Land and the National Question in Ireland,*
          1858-1882. Humanities Press, Atlantic Highlands, New
          Jersey.
                  One of the first complete studies of the
          socioeconomic conditions that spawned an agrarian
          movement and lead to the destruction of colonial
          landlordism. It contains some material on the relationship
          of the movement to its American support groups.

40   Bisceglia, L.R. 1979. *The Fenian Funeral of Terrence Belew*
          McManus. Eire/Ireland. 14:3:45-64.
                  This article follows the controversial funeral of
          McManus from San Francisco (Jan 1861) to its culmination
          in Dublin 11 months later. It discusses how the turmoil
          surrounding the event contributed to and influenced Irish
          nationalist politics and the spirit of Fenianism.

41   _____. 1981. The McManus Welcome, San Francisco, 1851.
          Eire/Ireland, 16:1:6-20.
                  Discusses the importance of the role Terrence
          Belew McManus played in the San Francisco Irish
          community. His arrival coincided with the formation and
          growth in power of Irish-American organizations. He
          represented a symbol of persistence against British rule as
          well as the spirit of his adopted city. It documents the
          nature of San Francisco's welcome for this escapee from a
          British penal colony in Tasmania.

42   Brannigan, C.J. 1977. The Luke Dillon Case and the
          Welland Canal Explosion of 1900: Non-Events in the

History of the Niagara Frontier Region. *Niagara Frontier*, 24:2:36-44.

A discussion of the conviction and imprisonment of Dillon and 2 others (Walsh & Nolan) for an unsuccessful attempt to destroy a lock in Welland Canal in Canada. Dillon maintained his innocence but was convicted on flimsy evidence and served the longest sentence of the three. It documents Clan na Gael's attempts to secure Dillon's release.

43   Brundage, D. 1986. Irish Land and American Workers: Class and Ethnicity in Denver Colorado. In: *Struggle A Hard Battle*. D. Hoerder, ed. University of Illinois Press, Champaign, Illinois. Pp. 46-67.

A brief article on Irish labor union activism in the Denver area and its relation to Irish nationalist activity in the area. It contains significant information on the Land League and its class composition.

44   Buckley, B.C. 1973. *The Fenians and Anglo-American Relations After the Civil War.* Kansas State University. Masters Thesis.

A study of how Fenianism effected Anglo-American relations and how the issues raised or complicated by Fenianism were ultimately resolved. The author feels that the Fenians exploited America's anglophobia as well as actual diplomatic problems between the British and the Americans such as the Alabama Claims, the San Juan Islands dispute and the Canadian fisheries issue. He also feels that the Fenians and the threat of war in Europe with Prussia made the English anxious to settle their problems with the States. The Fenian inspired naturalization issue eventually played a significant part in the reapproachment between the two countries.

45   Cahill, K.M. 1984. A Fenian Physician. In: *The American Irish Revival*. K.M. Cahill, ed. Associated Faculty Press, Port Washington, New York. pp. 244-252.

A brief biographical sketch of Dr. Patrick McCartan a physician member of Clan na Gael and tireless worker for Irish freedom in both Philadelphia and his native Ireland during the early 20th century. After independence he returned to Ireland and remained prominent in Irish nationalist politics until his death in 1963.

46   Cassidy, M.A. 1941. *The History of the Fenian Movement in the United States, 1848-1866, and Its Background in Ireland and America*. University of Buffalo, Masters Thesis.

A hard to obtain thesis which attempts to describe the origins and development of the Fenian movement from an Irish-American perspective. The author tries to reveal the connections between revolutionary societies in Ireland and the United States. It is based largely on an examination of the papers of General Thomas W. Sweeny which included correspondence, newspaper files, quartermaster records, field notes, lists of personnel, Fenian circles and other organizational materials.

47   Clark, D.I. 1970. *Letters from the Underground: The Fenian Correspondence of James Gibbons*. Records of American Catholic Historical Society, Philadelphia. 81:83-88.

A brief chronology of the correspondence of James Gibbons a member of the Fenian Brotherhood from Philadelphia. A good reference source for further content analysis of his letters.

48   _____. 1971. Militants of the 1860's: The Philadelphia Fenians. *Pennsylvania Magazine History and Biography,* 95:98-108.

A brief but well done analysis of the successes and difficulties of the Philadelphia Fenians in the 1860's, with interesting connections to the Catholic Church.

49   Clark, S. 1979. *Social Origins of the Irish Land War*. Princeton University, Princeton, New Jersey.

A study of the origins of the Irish Land War of

1879-1882 in context of the changing social structure of colonial Ireland during the nineteenth century. It includes some references to the American connections of the Irish Land League.

50   Comerford, R.V. 1985. *The Fenians in Context*. Wolfhound Press, Dublin.

A well documented work that attempts to examine Fenianism in the context of the political and social history of mid Victorian Ireland. It also traces the historic development of Fenianism from the Young Irelanders to the Land League. It includes material on American participation including the emergence and contributions of the Clan na Gael.

51   Connor, C.P. 1984. *Archbishop Hughes and the Question of Ireland, 1820-1862*. Records of American Catholic Historical Society of Philadelphia 95:1-4:15-26.

A discuss of Archbishop Hughes views on the Irish question and his commitment to peaceful solutions and the ongoing struggles of radical Irish militants. It also discusses his opposition to western colonialization by the Irish in America and his views toward assimilation with retention of strong ethnic pride.

52   Conway, K.E. 1891. John Boyle O'Reilly. *The Catholic World*, 53:211-216.

An extended review essay by a sympathetic reviewer based on *The Life of John Boyle O'Reilly* a book by James Jeffrey Roche.

53   Creigton, R.J. 1882. Influence of Foreign Issues on American Politics. *International Review*, 13:182-190.

A plea for immigrants to leave their grievances in the mother country. His major agenda is an attack on the Irish Land League's intrusion into the United States. A decidedly pro-British attack on American intervention in Ireland.

54   Cuddy, H. 1953. *The Influence of the Fenian Movement on
        Anglo-American Relations, 1860-1872.* St. John's University.
        Ph.D. Dissertation.
                A study of the impact of the Fenian movement on
        Anglo-American relations during a time period when the
        United States and Britain were not friendly. It includes a
        detailed discussion of the Naturalization Controversy and the
        Naturalization Treaty of 1870, as well as the Alabama Claims
        issue. A good source of material for a ten year period when
        the Fenians caused serious difficulties between the United
        States and Britain.

55   D'Arcy, W. 1947. *The Fenian Movement in the United
        States, 1858-1886.* Catholic University, Washington, D.C.
        (Reprinted, 1971, Russell & Russell, New York)
                A detailed history of the Fenian movement in the
        U.S. based in large part on the O'Mahoney-Rossa papers
        and the diplomatic correspondence between the United
        States and Britain during the years 1865-70. It attempts to
        explain the Fenians in the context of the politics of the post-
        Civil War period and the fact that England attempted to
        actively influence the outcome of the American Civil War.

56   Davitt, M. 1904. *The Fall of Feudalism in Ireland.* Harper,
        New York.
                Davitt's classic work on the destruction of the
        landlord system in Ireland, a must to understand the nature
        of the Land War and Irish Land League.

57   Delury, J.F. 1986. Irish Nationalism in the Sacramento
        Region (1850-1890). *Eire-Ireland*, 21:3:27-54.
                A brief history of the how, when and why of Irish
        settlement in the Sacramento region. Discusses a variety of
        Irish-American organizations in the area and how they
        served the cause. It includes material on the Fenians, Land
        League, Irish Republican Brotherhood (IRB), Clan na Gael,
        as well as, state militia, benevolent associations and relief
        organizations.

58   Denieffe, J. 1904. *A Personal Narrative of the Irish Revolutionary Brotherhood.* The Gael, New York. (Reprinted 1969, Irish University Press, Shannon, Ireland)

The personal recollections of the first decade of the Irish Republican Brotherhood from 1855-1867. Joseph Denieffe was the envoy from New York to the IRB in Ireland and was present at the founding of the IRB. Denieffe only covers operations and matters he was directly involved with. A valuable document appendix of over 130 pages is also included. The reprint edition includes a critical introduction by Sean O'Luing.

59   Devoy, J. 1878. Irish Comments on An English Text. *North American Review,* 147:281-285.

A journalistic attack on the Bayard-Chamberlain Extradition Treaty between the U.S. and Great Britain. It was so broad that it could be brought to bear on any Irish exile in the U.S. as an instrument of coercion.

60   Devoy, J. 1882. *The Land of Eire and the Irish Land League.* Patterson and Nelson, New York.

One of the most famous and persistent Irish-American rebels gives his interpretation of the effects of landlordism in Ireland and his solutions for the problem.

61   Devoy, J. 1929. *Recollections of an Irish Rebel.* Charles Young, New York. (Reprinted in 1969, Irish University Press, Dublin).

A collection of Devoy's recollections of the Irish nationalist movement from the mid 19th to the early 20th century. An excellent source on the Irish Republican Brotherhood, Fenianism and the Clan na Gael by a major participant. Devoy portrays the essential character and philosophy of Irish nationalism from the Fenians to the Rising of 1916. It includes a critical introduction by Sean O'Luing.

62   Devoy, J. 1948. *Devoy's Post Bag 1871-1928.* (2 Vols.) C.J.
         Fallon, Dublin.
                  A collection of selected letters and documents from
         John Devoy's personal papers from the 1870's to the Anglo-
         Irish War. These papers are of unique value for study of the
         growth and development of Irish nationalism up to partition
         and its American connections.

63   Donovan, H.D.A. 1930. Fenian Memories in Northern New
         York. *Journal American Irish History Society,* 28:148-152.
                  A very brief account of Fenian days around the
         village of Ft. Covington, New York during the summer of
         1870.

64   Edwards, O.D.   1967.   American Diplomats and Irish
         Coercion, 1880-83. *Journal of American Studies*, 1:2:213-232.
                  A discussion of American diplomatic reactions to
         the passage of the Coercion Act of 1881 which gave Britain
         power to imprison anyone on suspicion of committing or
         being likely to commit offenses against law and order and
         hold them without trial. The Act resulted in a number of
         naturalized American citizens being jailed without trial for
         Land League activity. A strong commentary on the pro-
         British bias of our State Department.

65   Ellis, P.B. 1986. The Battle of Ridgeway, 2 June 1886. *Irish
         Sword*, 16:65:245-267.
                  A detailed analysis of the Battle of Ridgeway during
         the Fenian invasions which the author views as a Fenian
         success. The article also discusses the idea that Fenian
         invasion may have been strongly responsible for the
         emergence of a new government in Canada.

66   Emmet, T.A.J. 1911. *Incidents of My Life.* Putnam, New
         York.
                  The personal memoirs of a United Irishman who
         fled to the United States after the Rising of 1798.

67   Finerty, J.F.   1893.   Thirty Years of Ireland's Battle.
        Donahoe's Magazine, 30:65-71.
                The reminiscences of a Fenian about the Fenian
        organization and its internal stresses. A good source for the
        names of Fenian leaders in the midwest such as Father
        O'Flaherty from Indiana.

68   Foner, E.   1978.   Class, Ethnicity and Radicalism in the
        Gilded Age: The Land League and Irish America. *Marxist
        Perspectives,* 2:6-55.
                An excellent study that perceives Irish-American
        nationalism as an expression of working class radicalism,
        especially in relation to its connections with the labor
        movement. Foner calls for a reevaluation of the whole field
        of Irish-American working class radicalism which has been
        ignored or downplayed by most historians. An excellent
        source of material on the Irish Land League, Clan na Gael
        and the relationship of the labor movement to Irish-
        American nationalism.

69   Ford, P.   1888.   The Irish Vote in the Pending Presidential
        Election. *North American Review,* 147:185-190. (August)
                An article in which Patrick Ford accused the Irish
        in America of blindly supporting British Free Trade which
        had destroyed Irish industries and forced many to emigrate.
        He urged support of the American economic system not the
        British colonial system.

70   Funchion, M.F.   1973.   *Chicago's Irish Nationalists, 1881-
        1890.*   Loyola University, Chicago.   Ph.D. Dissertation.
        (Reprinted 1976. *Chicago's Irish Nationalists.* Arno Press,
        New York)
                A scholarly history of Irish-American nationalist
        activity in Chicago as part of their own quest for
        respectability. It traces the growth and ultimately the
        destruction of the Clan na Gael in Chicago. The most
        detailed extant study of the Clan na Gael and its quest for
        Irish freedom. It is a rich source of bibliographical

resources.

71   ____. 1975. Irish Nationalists and Chicago's Politics in the 1880's. *Eire/Ireland*, 10:2:3-18.
     A study of the Clan na Gael involvement in Chicago politics, illustrates how Irish-America nationalism was often tied up with local politics. It also suggests how local disputes, scandals and economic interests were able to disrupt the nationalist aspect of the movement.

72   ____. 1981. Irish Chicago Church, Homeland Politics and Class in the Shaping of an Ethnic Group 1870-1900. In: *Ethnic Chicago*. Holi, P.G. and P. Jones, eds. Wm Eerdmans, Grand Rapids. Pp. 8-39.
     An excellent synthesis of the relationship of the Catholic Church, Chicago politics and Irish-American nationalism. An interesting contrast to the development of Irish nationalism in the East coast Irish centers. A well organized piece with lots of facts, interconnections and fresh interpretations.

73   George, J., Jr. 1981. Very Rev. Dr. Patrick E. Moriatrty, O.S.A. Philadephia's Fenian Spokesman. *Pennsylvania History*, 48:221-233.
     A brief but interesting study of Rev. Patrick Moriarty, OSA an Irish priest who rallied to the Fenian cause. It documents the rift between him and the Catholic hierarchy over Fenianism as well as the attempt by Bishop Word to revoke his priestly power. But Moriarty remained a devoted defender of the Irish struggle against England till his death in 1875.

74   Green, E.R.R. 1958. Fenians. *History Today*, 8:698-705.
     A brief, well written article on the history of Fenianism from the Young Irelanders of 1848 to the Fenian Rising and its Irish-American support.

75   Green, P.M. 1981. Irish Chicago: The Multiethnic Road to
          Machine Success. In: *Ethnic Chicago*. P. Jones and M.F.
          Holli ed. Wm B. Eeerdmans Publishing Co. Grand Rapids,
          Michigan.
                  An article that primarily deals with the rather
          unique development of Chicago machine politics and its Irish
          connection. However, it integrates significant material on
          the interconnection between Irish-American nationalism and
          Chicago politics.

76   Green, J.J. 1949. American Catholics and the Irish Land
          League, 1879-1922. *Catholic Historical Review*, 35:19-42.
                  Discusses the support for the Irish Land League
          among the American Catholic clergy and their parishioners.
          It also presents a detailed chronology of the growth and
          development of the Land League in the United States, well
          documented with primary sources.

77   Guptill, P.F. 1969. A Popular Bibliography of the Fenian
          Movement. *Eire/Ireland*, 4:2:18-25.
                  A bibliography of sources on the Fenian Movement,
          including a list of papers and personal memoirs.

78   Hanna, W.F. 1985. The Rescue of John Boyle O'Reilly.
          Log of Mystic Seaport, 36:4:126-132.
                  A brief account of the escape of an Irish rebel from
          a British prison in Western Australia and his flight on the
          ship, Gazelle, and other vessels to Boston.

79   Harmon, M. ed. 1968. *Fenians and Fenianism*. University
          of Washington, Seattle.
                  A series of essays by Irish, Canadian, British and
          American scholars on various aspects of Fenianism such as
          the relationship with the church, poetry and oral tradition,
          republican ideology and its context in world history. The
          authors represent a variety of ideological interpretations of
          Fenianism.

80   Hazel, M.V. 1980. First Link: Parnell's American Tour,
         1880. *Eire/Ireland*, 15:1:6-24.
              A discussion of Parnell's third tour to the United
         States which was very successful both politically and
         financially. Financially a great deal of money was raised for
         relief and politically both Parnell and the Irish struggle were
         greatly enhanced. He addressed state legislatures and the
         U.S. Congress, met governors and cabinet members, even
         President Hayes and received tumultuous welcomes
         wherever he went in the United States. It is also a useful
         study of foreign politicians trying to negotiate the minefield
         of Irish-American nationalist political divisions or camps.

81   Hernon, J.M. 1964. The Use of the American Civil War in
         the Debate Over Irish Home Rule. *American Historical
         Review*, 69:4:1022-1026.
              A brief note that considers the views of radical
         republicans and liberal unionists in England on a comparison
         of the American Civil War and Irish Home Rule issue.

82   _____. 1966. The Irish Nationalists and the Southern
         Seccession. *Civil War History*, 4:43-53:
              An attempt to show that the Irish were not
         monolithic in their support for the Union over the
         Confederates. It considers ambiguities and changing
         patterns of support for the Union among the Irish.
         However, the data used is selective and taken out of context
         in an effort to counteract the mythology of total Irish
         support for the North over the British supported South.

83   _____. 1968. *Celts, Catholics and Copperheads: Ireland
         Views the American Civil War*. Ohio State University Press,
         Columbus.
              An interesting monograph that presents the authors
         hypotheses that the American Civil War presented a
         dilemma for many Irish nationalists. It is an antidote to the
         popular myth that the Irish must have supported the Union
         because the British supported the Confederacy.

84   Hill, H.W. 1921. The Fenian Raid of '66. *Buffalo Historical Society Publications*, 25:263-285.
        A good account of the invasion from Buffalo and of conditions there before and after the attempt. It does show that the Fenians had support in Buffalo.

85   Hoslett, S.D. 1940. The Fenian Brotherhood. *Americana*, 34:596-603.
        A brief history of the growth and development of the Fenian Brotherhood in America and its relationship with the United States government until the Anglo-American Treaty of 1870.

86   Hunt, H.M. 1889. *The Crime of the Century or the Assassination of Dr. Patrick Henry Cronin*. Kochersperger, Chicago.
        The author, a journalist, attempts to present a complete, chronological narrative of the assassination of Dr. Patrick Cronin, a Chicago Clan na Gael leader.

87   Hurst, J.W. 1969. The Fenians: A Bibliography. *Eire/Ireland*, 4:4:90-106.
        A well organized bibliography of published sources of information on the Fenians.

88   James, H. 1880. *The Work of the Irish Leagues*. Cassell & Co, London.
        The speech of Sir Henry James on the Irish Leagues, as part of the Parnell Commission Inquiry of Sept 17, 1888 to Nov 22, 1889. The speech took 12 days to deliver and this large volume was produced from the official notes of the Inquiry. It is a decidedly pro-British analysis of the origin, principles and action of the activities of the Irish Leagues in Ireland and the United States. It is really a parliamentary intelligence report on Irish and Irish-American insurgency during the late 19th century. It includes much material on Michael Davitt and Charles Parnell in America as well as the operation of the Clan na Gael. This is a

compendium of British fears, bigotry and cultural attitudes with respect to the Irish struggle for both land reform and political freedom. It is very useful for capturing the tone of British upper class feelings towards Ireland and Irish issues.

89   Jenkins, B. 1968. The British Government, Sir John A. MacDonald, and the Fenian Claims. *Canadian History Review*, 41:142-159.
         A discussion of the Canadian government attempts to gain compensation from both U.S. and Britain for the actions of the Fenians. The British were cited because it was the British connection that led to the raids. It also discusses the role of Sir John A. MacDonald the Canadian prime minister as a negotiator who ran into a political mine field.

90   ____. 1969. *Fenians and Anglo-American Relations During Reconstruction*. Cornell University, Ithaca.
         A scholarly monograph that deals with the diplomatic influence of the Fenian movement on Anglo-Irish relations during the six years following the Civil War. It is a well documented work based on a wide variety of primary source materials from the U.S., Canada, England and Ireland. A detailed, well written story that chronicles the role of ethnicity in foreign affairs.

91   Kenneally, J.J. 1986. Sexism, the Church, and Irish Women. *Eire/Ireland*, 21:3:3-16.
         An interesting article on the tendency to ignore the Irish woman's contribution to history. Kenneally shows how many Irish-American women engaged in activities that enraged the Church. Among these activities were the labor movement and the struggle between Bishop Gilmour of Cleveland and the Ladies Land League which form the core of the paper.

92   Kiernan, J.L. 1864. *Ireland and America, Versus England, From a Fenian Point of View*. G.W. Pattison. Detroit.

A pamphlet based on a lecture by Brig. Gen. J.L. Kiernan, U.S.A., given in the principal towns and cities of the west such as Detroit, Saginaw, Michigan, Lafayette, Indiana, Springfield, Illinois, Cincinnati, and Indianapolis. It was authorized by the Fenian Brotherhood in an effort to demonstrate what Fenianism really is and ultimately to aid its advancement.   An interesting example of political oriented public speaking.

93   King, C.L. 1909. The Fenian Movement. *University of Colorado Studies*, 6:187-213.
A detailed article that attempts to view the Fenian Movement from its roots in the Famine and the Young Ireland Movement of 1846-48 through its official organization and its successes and failures. It discusses the role of American politics in the Fenian movement and how the U.S. Government used it to force concessions by the British.

94   King, J.A. 1988. The Fenian Invasion of Canada and John McMahon: Priest, Saint, and Charlatan.   *Eire/Ireland*, 23:4:32-51.
A interesting discussion of a Fenian enigma, John McMahon, who was jailed in Canada for 3 year after the Battle of Ridgeway.   He claimed to be a priest falsely arrested after he was at Ridgeway by chance not choice. However he did do his "Christian duty" as priest and nurse. After leaving prison he went on a lecture tour, speaking of his prison experiences, but eventually was reinstated as a priest in Reynolds, Indiana where he died in 1872. His real role in the Fenian movement if any is unclear but it's a nice human interest story.

95   Kraus, M. 1939. America and the Irish Revolutionary Movement in the Eighteenth Century. In: *The Era of The American Revolution*.   R.B. Morris, ed.   Columbia University, New York. Pp. 332-348.

A interesting essay on the interrelationships and similarities between the struggle for freedom in both Ireland and America at the time of the American Revolution.

96   Langan, M. 1937. *General John O'Neill Soldier, Fenian and Leader of Irish Catholic Colonization in America.* University of Notre Dame. Masters Thesis.

A short Masters Thesis on the life and contributions of John O'Neill, a Fenian who settled in Nebraska. It describes O'Neill's early life and his role in the Fenian invasions of Canada. It is especially good on O'Neill's late career as a colonizer in Nebraska's Holt and Greeley counties.

97   Laubenstein, W.J. 1960. *The Emerald Whaler: A Saga of the Sea and Men Who Risked All for Freedom.* Bobbs-Merrill. Indianapolis.

A popular account of the daring rescue of Fenian prisoners from a British prison in Fremantle, Australia by the American ship Catalpa. It is written in a narrative style that reads like a novel.

98   Luning, P. 1993. Irish Blood. *Chicago History*, 22:3:21-37.

Using the controvesy over the 1889 murder of Clan na Gael member Dr. Patrick Henry Cronin the article discusses the position of the Clan na Gael in Chicago as well as the debate over Irish-American loyalty to the United States. The author concludes that Irish-Americans weathered a storm of nationalist criticism related to their jealous Irish nationalism while strengthening their own ethnicity. Irish nationalism survived the Cronin scandal and devotion to Irish culture was greatly reinforced by the Irish community's examination of their position in America.

99   McEnnis, J.T. 1889. *The Clan na Gael and the Murder of Dr. Patrick Henry Cronin.* F.J. Schittze and J.W. Iliff. Chicago.

A contemporary account by John T. McEnnis a Clan na Gael member of the Sullivan wing and a newspaper reporter. He proposes that Cronin was killed in a fight after he tried to resist attempts to get him to turn over a minority report that accused the Sullivan group of falsifying accounts during 1881-84, as well other charges. It would seem Cronin also carried the report with him.

100   McGee, R.   1970.   *The Fenian Raids on the Huntington Frontier, 1866 and 1870.* R. McGee, Malone, New York.
        A brief monograph that describes the nature of the Fenian Raids into Canada along the northern New York frontier. It is very biased toward a Canadian or British viewpoint but does provide some interesting local details not generally found in the larger works on the Fenian movement.

101   McGee, T.D.   1866.   *The Irish Position in Britain and in Republican North America.* Longmoore, Montreal.
        A pamphlet that includes an attack on Fenianism, along with an unfavorable comparison between the position of the Irish in Canada and the United States. The American Irish come out on the short end. It includes a geographic survey of the Irish in Canada, a letter from the Irish bishop of Halifax, Thomas L. Connally, on Fenianism and a description of St. Patricks Day, 1866 in Montreal.

102   McManamin, F.G.   1959.   *The American Years of John Boyle O'Reilly, 1870-1890.* Catholic University Ph.D. Dissertation. (Reprinted, 1976 Arno Press).
        A study that traces the Irish activities of John Boyle O'Reilly in the United States. It examines his role as an Irish rebel, editor, literary figure, Catholic layman and a social reformer. It includes a valuable essay on research sources.

103   Mannion, L.F. (ed.).   1969.   Constitution and By Laws of the Fenian Brotherhood of Colorado Territory. *Eire/Ireland*, 4:2:7-17.

A reproduction of the preamble and articles 1 through 38 of the Fenian Brotherhood constitution and by-laws.

104   Minnick, W.C.   1953.   Parnell in America.   *Speech Monographs*, 20:38-48.

A discussion of Charles Stuart Parnell's speaking tour of America in 1880 to plead for American support for the abolition of landlordism in Ireland, which he believed was the cause of Ireland's poverty. Contrasts the hostility towards Parnell of the New York press with the positive reaction of the Midwestern press.

105   Mitchell, A.   1967.   The Fenian Movement in America. *Eire/Ireland*, 2:6-10.

A brief history of the development of the Fenian movement in America and the difficulties encountered with some emphasis on the raids on Canada and the United States government's attitude.

106   Montgomery, P.   1967.   *Beyond Equality: Labor and the Radical Republicans 1862-72.* Knopf, New York.

This work contains some interesting material on the relationships between the labor movement and Irish nationalism especially pages 127-134.

107   Moody, T.W.   1968. *The Fenian Movement.* Mercier, Cork, Ireland.

A collection of brief articles by a number of major Irish scholars ranging from the origin of the movement to a series of biographical sketches on seven major leaders, to the role of Fenianism in Irish history. A good introduction to the subject.

108   _____.   1981.   *Davitt and the Irish Revolution.*   Oxford University, London.

A comprehensive study of Michael Davitt and his impact on the Land War in Ireland. It has many references to the Irish-American connection. Chapters 7 and 10 consist of a detailed analysis of Michael Davitt's 1878 and 1880 trips to America and their impact on the course of the campaign against landlordism.

109   Moriarty, T.F. 1980. The Irish-American Response to Catholic Emancipation. *Catholic Historical Review*, 66:3:353-373.
       Discusses Irish-American support for Catholic Emancipation movement from 1823-1829. Emphasizes the generally positive response of both Irish Catholics and of Irish Protestants in the United States. The author also discusses the support of the press. However the author believes that the American campaign did more for the Irish in America than back home, promoting cooperation among the Irish and possibly stimulating the growth of Irish nationalism.

110   Morrow, R.L. 1934. The Negotiation for the Anglo-American Treaty of 1870. *American History Review*, 39:663-681.
       A discussion of the passage of a treaty that protected the legal rights of naturalized American citizens of Irish descent when travelling in the United Kingdom. It also relates the development of the treaty to the role of Fenian movement in Anglo-America relations.

111   Murphy, B. 1988. Father Peter Yorke's "Turning of the Tide" (1899): The Strictly Cultural Nationalism of the Early Gaelic League. *Eire/Ireland*, 23:1:35-44.
       A consideration of the mixed reception of Father Yorke's nationalism by the two sections of the Gaelic League, the separatists who wanted complete independence and the culturalists who simply wanted a Gaelic speaking nation. However, the author feels that Yorke's speech to the Gaelic League on Sept 6, 1899 was a major stimulus for the Gaelic League to move toward militant assertion of their right to independence.

112   Myers, P.E. 1981. The Fenians in Iowa. *Palimpsest*, 62:56-
       64.
              A brief description of Fenian activity in Iowa
       especially in areas with large Irish populations like Des
       Moines, Davenport and Iowa City. It also discuss the role
       of the Clan na Gael and Land League in Iowa.

113   Neidhardt, W.S. 1972. The American Government and the
       Fenian Brotherhood: A Study in Mutual Political
       Opportunism. *Ontario History*, 64:27-44.
              A well organized discussion of the Fenian threat to
       Canada, the early ambivalence of the United States
       government, the role of Fenian threat in gaining support for
       Canadian confederation and the reasons for the military
       failure of the movement.

114   _____. 1975. *Fenianism in North America*. Pennsylvania
       State University. State College, Pennsylvania.
              A study of the rise of Fenianism with a special
       emphasis on the invasion of Canada and its impact on
       Canadian nationalism. The author feels that the Fenian
       movement must be treated as a serious interlude in North
       American history and not dismissed in a cavalier manner as
       inconsequential.

115   Newsinger, J. 1980. John Mitchel and Irish Nationalism.
       Literature and History, 6:2:182-200.
              A well written article on John Mitchel and his
       nationalist ideology, his transportation and escape from Van
       Dieman's Land in July 1853. However, it contains material
       on Mitchel's seperatist position after residence in the United
       States as well as his reactionary racist approach to the
       slavery issue in the United States.

116   O'Broin, L. 1971. *Fenian Fever: An Anglo-American
       Dilemma*. New York University, New York.
              A scholarly monograph on the growth and
       development of Fenians in both Ireland and America. The

author presents interesting information on the Fenians within the British army and American soldiers from the Civil War as well as the insurrection and its aftermath.

117 ____. 1976. *Revolutionary Underground: The Story of the Irish Republican Brotherhood, 1859-1924.* Dublin, Gill and Macmillan.
A well written history of the Irish Republican Brotherhood the forerunner to the IRA, that considers the personalities, structural organization, internal problems and impact of the organization both in Ireland and America.

118 O'Cathaoir, B. 1985. Terence Bellow McManus, Fenian Precursor. *Irish Sword,* 16:63:105-109.
A brief background on McManus his conviction and transportation to Van Diemen's Land and eventual escape to the United States. It includes a letter written by McManus to John Blake Dillon (7/14/1851) concerning the still imprisoned William Smith O'Brien.

119 ____. 1990. *John Blake Dillon, Young Irelander.* Irish Academic Press, Dublin.
A biography based largely on primary sources in the Dillon Papers of a leading member of Young Ireland who escaped to the United States and worked as a lawyer. He later returned to Ireland and served in Parliament as a leader of the Irish Party.

120 O'Connell, M.R. 1981. Daniel O'Connell and Irish-Americans. *Eire/Ireland,* 16:2:7-15.
A study of O'Connell's differences with Irish-Americans on the issue of the abolition of slavery. It also includes a brief background on O'Connell's work in Ireland. It does not include much criticism of O'Connell's politics and motivations.

121 ____. 1988. O'Connell, Young Ireland and Negro Slavery: An Exercise in Romantic Nationalism. *Thought,* 64:253:130-

131.

A rather slanted consideration of O'Connell's enlightened idealism versus the Young Irelanders romantic nationalistic ideology in the context of the slavery issue in the United States. Young Irelanders are given no credit for condemning slavery since their motives were "political" but O'Connell's praised for holding the moral high ground.

122   O'Donnell, F.H.   1883.   Fenianism Past and Present. *Contemporary Review*, 43:747-766.

A brief history of the Fenian movement in Ireland and the United States. It relates both its victories and defeats. It also deals with the shift of the energies of many Fenians to the Land League.

123   O'Donovan-Rossa, J. 1898. *Rossa's Recollections 1858 to 1898*. Mariner's Harbor, New York.

The memories of the legendary Irish revolutionary who emigrated to America, Jeremiah O'Donovan Rossa. A rich source of primary material on social life in Ireland, prison life in England and the ideology and personal dedication of an old revolutionary. A revolutionary who had a great impact on the ideology of many Irish American nationalists even into the present time period.

124   O'Fahey, C.J. 1975. Reflections on the St. Patrick's Day Orations of John Ireland. *Ethnicity*, 2:3:244-257.

A discussion of the religious and cultural themes associated with the St. Patrick's Day orations of Archbishop John Ireland of St. Paul, Minn. Seven centuries of British oppression in Ireland was prominent among these orations. Many of these speeches served to sustain nationalistic aspirations among Irish-Americans.

125   O'Grady, J.P. 1958. *The Irish-American Influence in the Rejection of the Phelps-Rosebery Extradition Treaty of 1886*. University of Notre Dame. Masters Thesis.

A study of the extradition proposed by the American

minister to Britain Edward Phelps and Lord Rosebery. After two and a half years of heavy Irish-American opposition it was rejected by the Senate on January 31 1889. However, the author feels that American issues killed it, although the author concedes it is almost impossible to judge the impact of the Irish vote.

126   ____. 1965. *Irish-American and Anglo-American Relations, 1880-1888*. University of Pennsylvania. Ph.D. Dissertation. (reprinted 1976, Arno Press).
        A study that attempts to analyze Irish-American power in American politics and its ability to influence the Anglo-American relations. The author feels that Irish-Americans did not greatly influence the trend of Anglo-American relations during this period.

127   O'Keefe, T.J.   1984.   The Art and Politics of Parnell Monument. *Eire/Ireland*, 19:1:6-25.
        An article on the political reactions to the erection of a monument to Charles Parnell in Dublin proposed by John Redmond the leader of the Irish Parliamentary Party. It promoted a lot of animosity since many nationalists thought Redmond was trying to use the memory of Parnell to promote the Redmond faction in the United States where Parnell was revered. It includes a discussion of Redmond's visit to the U.S. to promote the idea and the reaction of Irish-Americans to such efforts.

128   O'Leary, J.A. 1896. *Recollections of Fenians and Fenianism*. 2 vols. Harpers, London. (reprint: 1969. Irish Universities Press, Dublin)
        An extensive collection of primary material on the Fenian movement and its ideology through the recollections of a major participant in the movement, John O'Leary a one time editor of *The Irish People* a Fenian newspaper. It includes a critical introduction by Marcus Bourke.

129   _____. 1919. *My Political Trials and Experience*. Jefferson
Publishing Co., NY.
           The story of the arrest, indictment and prolonged
imprisonment of Jeremiah A. O'Leary an American militant.
It is a story of intrigue by governments against an individual
deemed dangerous as well as the eventual collapse of the
corporation and the vindication of O'Leary by a jury trial in
a Federal Court.   It includes a biographical sketch of
O'Leary by Major Michael A. Kelly.

130   O'Luing, S. 1961. *John Devoy*. Anvil, Tralee, Ireland.
           A brief biography of John Devoy, a Fenian founder
of Clan na Gael and an ardent supporter of the Irish
nationalist cause in both America and Ireland until his death
in 1926.

131   _____. 1965. *The Fremantle Mission*. Anvil, Tralee, Ireland.
           A concise account of the rescue of six Fenian
prisoners from a British prison in Australia by the American
ship Catalpa in 1875-76.   It contains much analysis of the
Clan na Gael's role in the incident.

132   O'Neill, J. 1870. *Official Report of General John O'Neill,
President of the Fenian Brotherhood on the Attempt to Invade
Canada May 25, 1870*. New York.
           A detailed report of two attempts by the O'Neill
wing to annex Canada. It is especially valuable since O'Neill
comments on why the attempts failed.

133   O'Reilly, J.B. 1882. Ireland's Opportunity, Will it be Lost?
American Catholic Quarterly Review, 7:114-120.
           O'Reilly proposes that 1882 should be the year that
the Irish band together and demand that Ireland have its
own government.   He felt that if the demand was not
pressed now, the opportunity would be lost and the Land
League would dwindle into insignificance.

134   _____. 1886. At Last. *North American Review*, 142:104-110.

He feels the exiles of the Great Famine in the O'Reilly recounts the history of British oppression in Ireland from the 12th centruy to the rise of Irish Party in Paliament. He feels the exiles of the Great Famine in the United States and other lands have created strong pressure on England. He predicts that 1889, will be the year for the repeal of union.

135   O'Rourke, H.E. 1989. The Union Club Riot of Thanksgiving Day 1920. *New York Irish History*, 16-19.

A description of a riot that occurred in New York in 1920 when the pro-British Union Club across from St. Patrick's Cathedral flew the Union Jack on a day when a memorial mass for Terence MacSwiney, the Lord Mayor of Cork and hunger strike victim, was being held at St. Patrick's. It concludes that the Union Club was trying to provoke a reaction from the mourners and got more than they bargained for.

136   Patrick, J.J. 1983-84. The Cleveland Fenians: A Study in Ethnic Leadership. *The Old Northwest*, 9:4:307-327.

An interesting study of Fenian Brotherhood in Cleveland and its effects on local politics, ethnic identities as well as support for Irish nationalism. It traces the development of the movement and its eventual split and the effects of the split on the Irish population of Cleveland.

137   Pease, Z.Q. and G.S. Anthony. 1897. *The Catalpa Expedition*. G.S. Anthony, New Bedford, Massachuettes.

An account of the rescue of Fenian prisoners from an Australian prison, by the Catalpa in an expedition organized by Clan na Gael. It is based on the recollections of the commander of the Catalpa, Captain George S. Anthony.

138   Pieper, E.H. 1931. *The Fenian Movement*. University of Illinois. Ph.D. Dissertation.

This study traces the origins, organization and development of the Fenian Brotherhood in the United States. It includes a detailed consideration of the split in the movement over whether to invade Canada or not. There is also a detailed discussion of the various attempts to invade Canada as well as the movement of some Fenians to Ireland for purposes of revolt. The research is based on U.S. Department of State files and the papers and newspaper coverage of both wings of the Brotherhood.

139   Potter, G. 1960. The Birth of Fenianism. In: *To the Golden Door*. G. Potter. Greenwood Press, Westport, Connecticut. Pp. 554-574.
A brief chronological history of the founding and growth of the Fenian movement in the United States and Ireland.

140   _____. 1960. The '98 Exiles and Catholic Emancipation. In: *To The Golden Door*. G. Potter. Greenwood Press, Westport, Connecticut. Pp. 207-216.
A description of the work of William Sampson, Dr. William J. MacNeven and Thomas Addis Emmet all exiles from the 1798 rising in marshalling support in 1825 for the Daniel O'Connell emancipation movement.

141   _____. 1960. The Riven Repeal Agitation. In: *To The Golden Door*. G. Potter. Greenwood Press, Connecticut. Pp. 387-404.
A description of American activity associated with the founding O'Connell's repeal movement in Ireland in 1840. A good source of popular reaction as well as those of contemporary politicians on the eastern seaboard to Irish issues.

142   _____. 1960. The Widow McCormick's Cabbage Patch. In: *To the Golden Door*. G. Potter. Greenwood Press, Westport, Connecticut. Pp. 498-507.v
A brief description of the American excitement and

expectations surrounding the Young Irelanders aims to free Ireland as well their hopes for the success of an armed insurrection.

143   Quinn, P.A. 1984. John Devoy: Recollection of an Irish Rebel. In: *The American Irish Revival*. K.M. Cahill, ed. Associated Faculty Press, Port Washington, New York. Pp. 231-243.
        A brief popular article that provides a quick chronology of the nationalist career of John Devoy.

144   Quinlivan, P. and P. Rose. 1982. *The Fenians in England 1865-1872*. Riverrun Press, New York.
        A well documented account of Fenian operations in England with some references to American involvement. It includes an excellent bibliography.

145   Redpath, J. 1881. *Talks About Ireland*. P.J. Kenedy, New York.
        A collection of lectures and articles from a number of American and Irish papers, that deal with Irish issues of the late 19th century. The topics range from famines and the priests to Parnell and his associates and landlords and land leagues.

146   Reeves, C.E. 1968. Davitt's American Tour of 1882. *Quarterly Journal of Speech*, 54:357-362.
        An interesting analysis of Michael Davitt's American tour of 1882 which was aimed at reunification of the Land League in the U.S. as well as raising money to finance its efforts in Ireland. This study examines Davitt's speaking style and how he won the public over to his cause through his speeches and ability to never dodge the tough issues brought up by his critics. It highlights Davitt's integrity, clarity, brightness and humor which never left a doubt where he stood.

147   Reidy, J. 1922. John Devoy. *Journal of American Irish Historical Society*, 27:413-425.
        A biographical sketch of the life and accomplishments of John Devoy, a Fenian and leader of the Clan na Gael, as well as the editor of *The Gaelic American* an Irish-American and Irish-American nationalist newspaper.

148   Reuter, W.C. 1979. The Anatomy of Political Anglophobia in the U.S., 1865-1900. *Mid-America*, 61:2:117-132.
        A study that analyzes American anglophobia as a serious political issue originating in the reality of the rivalry between the U.S. and Great Britain. It repeats the traditional view of many historians that anglophobia was an inane sideshow. It includes material on the contribution of Irish-Americans to Anglophobia and its influence on the Irish vote.

149   Robinson, D. (ed.) 1912. Fenians in South Dakota. In: *South Dakota Historical Collection*, 6:117-130.
        A collection of correspondence regarding the Fenian raid on Canada and a brief biographical sketch of Fenian General John O'Neill. Includes correspondence from General Winfield Hancock, A.T.A Kerman, Warren Cowles, George H. Williams, Doane Robinsin, J.A. Fowles and General John O'Neill.

150   Rosen, R. 1979. The Catalpa Rescue. *Journal of the Royal Australian Historical Society*, 65:2:73-88.
        A detailed description of the how, where, when and who of the escape of six Fenian prisoners from a British jail in Australia. An interesting commentary on a daring project that included 68 branches of the Clan na Gael and over 7000 men without any important leaks to the British authorities.

151   Ryan, D. 1937. *The Phoenix Flame: A Study of Fenianism and John Devoy*. Barker, London.
        One the earliest scholarly studies of the Fenian movement and an essential starting point for work in this

area. It is based in large part on Devoy's autobiography, *Recollections of an Irish Rebel*.

152   ____. 1969. *The Fenian Chief: A Biography of James Stephens*. University of Miami Press, Coral Gables, Florida.

A study of James Stephens based on Stephens' papers and his American diary. The American diary excerpts give insight into the culture of Irish revolutionary exiles and Stephens' reaction to it. The book was prepared for publication after Ryan's death by Owen Dudley Edwards but it is based wholly on Ryan's research.

153   Sammon, P.J. 1951. *The History of the Irish National Federation of America*. Masters Thesis. Catholic University.

The history of an organization that worked in America between 1891 and 1900 in the cause of home rule. It considers the role of the organization in bringing the Irish cause before the American public as well as its financial support for the Evicted Tenants Fund and the Nationalist Party.

154   Savage, J. 1868. *Fenian Heroes and Martyrs*. P. Donahoe, Boston.

A compendium of brief biographical sketches of many of the Fenian leaders and their activities, in both Ireland and America. Very rich in nationalist popular history.

155   Schneirov, R. 1984. *The Knights of Labor in the Chicago Labor Movement and in Municipal Politics 1877-1887*. Northern Illinois University. Ph.D. Dissertation.

Primarily a study of the labor radicalism of the Knights of Labor in Chicago, but includes much material on the Irish Land League, the Fenians and Clan na Gael. The author considers the role that Irish nationalism played in the creation of American working class political culture.

156   Schofield, W.G. 1956. *Seek For a Hero - The Story of John Boyle O'Reilly*. Kennedy, New York.
        A shallow biography that really adds nothing new to our understanding of John Boyle O'Reilly.

157   Self, E. 1883. The Abuse of Citizenship. *North American Review*, 136:541-556.
        A criticism of the Irish nationalist campaign that reflects American fear of foreign involvement as well as anti-Irish immigrant bias. It is laced with anti-Irish invective and probably expressive of the isolationist attitudes of many Americans of this time period.

158   Senior, H. 1978. *The Fenians and Canada*. Macmillan, Toronto.
        This work presents a Canadian view of the Fenians. It attempts to analyze the Fenian invasion of Canada within the context of 19th century American politics and Anglo-American relations.

159   Short, K.R.M. 1979. *The Dynamite War: Irish-American Bombers in Victorian Britain*. Humanities Press, Atlantic Highlands, New Jersey.
        A scholarly study of the bombing campaign in British cities in the 1880's which was largely lead and financed by Irish-American nationalists. It contains much information of two Irish-American nationalist groups Jeremiah O'Donovan Rossa's "Skirmishers" and John Devoy's Clan na Gael. It is also an interesting examination of security response especially the British Secret Service and Scotland Yard. It begs comparison with the present bombing campaigns in Britain associated with the Irish Republican Army.

160   Sowles, E.A. 1880. History of Fenianism and Fenian Raids in Vermont. *Vermont Historical Society Proceedings*. pp. 67-79.

A brief history of the Fenian raids in Vermont by a local who supported the Fenians right to attack Canada. However it is based on his own memory not documentation.

161 Stockley, W.F.P. 1935. Reminiscences of John Boyle O'Reilly, 1844-1890. *Catholic World*, 140:664-72, 141:73-81.

A two part tribute to the life of John Boyle O'Reilly and his contributions to Irish life in America.

162 Strum, H. 1981. Federalist Hibernophobes in New York, 1807. *Eire/Ireland*, 16:4:7-13.

A short article that contains some references to Federalist connections with Toryism and Federalist fear of the Irish. It also discusses their political opponents identification of the Irish struggle with the American Revolution against British rule.

163 Sullivan, A. 1884. The American Republic and the Irish National League of America. *American Catholic Quarterly Review*, 9:35-44.

A lengthy defense of the Irish National Land League of America in reply to public criticism of that organization. It includes a detailed historical background on the nature of British exploitation in Ireland that has led to much Irish emigration to the United States. The author includes an interesting section on the positive benefits to the United States of Irish-American participation in the ideology and activities of the League.

164 Sweeny, T.W. 1866. *Official Report of General Thomas W. Sweeny, Secretary of War for the Fenian Brotherhood and Commander in Chief of the Irish Republican Army.* American Irish Historical Society, New York.

A report by Sweeny on the reasons for failure of commanders to furnish the number of troops promised. He also criticizes the American government for stopping reinforcements from reaching the invaders of Canada.

165   Sweeny, W.M. 1924. The Fenian Invasion of 1866. *Journal American Irish Historical Society*, 23:193-203.
          The son of the Fenian Thomas Sweeny discusses the Fenian invasion and why it failed.

166   Taylor, J.M. 1978. Fenian Raids Against Canada. *American History Illustrated*, 13:5:32-39.
          A well written popular description of the planning and implementation of the Fenian invasions of Canada in 1866.

167   Toner, P.M. 1981. The "Green Ghost": Canada's Fenians and The Raids. *Eire/Ireland*, 16:4:27-47.
          An interesting article that examines Canadian support for the Fenians as well as the relationship between Canadian and American Fenianism. It includes useful material on individual Canadian Fenians and their American connection.

168   Walker, M.G. 1969. *The Fenian Movement*. Ralph Myles, Colorado Springs, Colorado.
          A readable account heavily based on newspaper accounts of the organization and operation of the Fenian Brotherhood in American. It includes much useful material on factionalization within the Brotherhood.

169   Walsh, V.A. 1985. Irish Nationalism and Land Reform: The Role of the Irish in America. In: *The Irish in America: Emigration, Assimilation and Impact*. P.J. Drudy, ed. Cambridge University, New York. Pp. 253-270.
          An excellent analysis of the rise of Irish-American nationalism during the Fenian and Land War periods. It includes valuable criticisms of the theories of Thomas Brown and Eric Foner on the roots of Irish nationalism.

170   Welch, G.P. 1958. The Fenian Foray into Canada. *An Cosantoir*, 18:268-90, 290-301.

A detailed journalistic type military description of the Fenian invasion of Canada from Buffalo. It also includes some discussion of the long term ramifications of the failed invasion. An interesting report by someone with military expertise as well as sound historical knowledge.

171   Winkler, L. 1936. *The Fenian Movement and Anglo-American Diplomacy in the Reconstruction Period.* New York University. Masters Thesis.

A well cited Master Thesis that is apparently no longer available for study, even from the degree granting institution, New York University.

172   Wittke, C. 1956. The Fenian Fiasco. In: *The Irish in America.* C. Wittke. Russell and Russell, New York. Pp. 150-160.

A chapter in a general work on the Irish-American experience that gives a brief but interesting overview of the Fenian episode in American history.

CHAPTER 3

REVOLUTION AND PARTITION 1900-1960S

173   Bisceglia, L.R. 1982. Primary Sources of Anti-English
Activities in California, 1916-1936:   The John Byrne
Collection. *Southern California Quarterly*, 64:3:227-237.

A brief but important research article that highlights
the significance of the John Byrne Collection at San Jose
Library for studies of Irish-American nationalism for the
period   of   1916-1936.   It   discusses   Irish-American
organizations and the important people associated with them.
It also includes an extensive bibliography on California Irish-
American nationalism.

174   Blake, N.M.   1935.   *The United States and the Irish
Revolution 1914-1922.* Clark University. Ph.D. Dissertation.

A study of the history of Irish-American nationalism
in relation to British policies in Ireland, Sinn Fein tactics and
strategy   and   the   choice   between   isolationism   and
internationalism. It also considers the ups and downs of
American opinion in response to events in Ireland.   The
author feels that Woodrow Wilson was sympathetic to Irish
independence but fearful of his powerful British allies.   The
study also concludes that most Irish-Americans were
isolationists before, during and after World War I due to the
fact that the alternative would be an alliance with their
ancient English enemies. This is a useful study of a decade
of Irish-American activity and ideology related to Anglo-Irish
relations.

175   Brindley, R. 1988. Woodrow Wilson, Self-Determination
       and Ireland 1918-1919: A View from the Irish Newspapers.
       Eire/Ireland, 23:4:62-80.
              The role Irish newspapers played in the coverage of
       Wilson's proposal for ethnic self-determination and the
       Versailles Peace Conference after World War I. In spite of
       Wilson's failures the Irish press let him off the hook. Blame
       was placed on Lloyd George, the British Prime Minister for
       the exclusion of Ireland from the Peace Conference. In
       Ireland Wilson was still highly thought of after the Peace
       Conference, unlike America where he was despised by Irish-
       Americans.

176   Bromage, M.S. 1951. De Valera Mission to America.
       South Atlantic Quarterly, 50:499-513.
              Discusses De Valera's mission to gain financial,
       moral, and political support for Irish self-determination. It
       considers both his supporters and detractors in the United
       States.

177   Buckley, J.P. 1974. *The New York Irish: Their View of
       American Foreign Policy 1914-1921*. New York University.
       Ph. D. Dissertation. (Reprinted by Arno Press in 1976).
              A historical analysis of the participation of New
       York Irish in the fight for Irish independence during its most
       crucial years (1914-1921). It emphasizes the pivotal role of
       Daniel Cohalan, John Devoy, Jeremiah O'Leary and Robert
       and Austin Ford, as well as, *The Irish World* and *The Gaelic
       American* newspapers. It also, documents the constant
       attempt to influence American foreign policy on behalf of
       the Irish people, as well as, the Irish-American struggle with
       Woodrow Wilson in the aftermath of World War I. The
       struggle for control between Judge Cohalan and De Valera
       is considered in light of its impact on Irish-American
       influence. It relies heavily on an extensive examination of
       the private papers of Irish-American leaders and a survey of
       the Irish and Catholic newspapers and periodicals of the
       period.

178   Bunting, A. 1988. The American Molly Childers and the
        Irish Question. *Eire/Ireland*, 23:2:88-103.
                An interpretive article on the role of the American
        born widow of Erskine Childers in the struggle for Irish
        independence.

179   Carroll, F.M.   1978.   *American Opinion and the Irish
        Question 1910-1923*. St. Martins Press, New York.
                A comprehensive study of how the Irish-American
        community and its American allies influenced the struggle
        for Irish independence in the early twentieth century. It
        emphasizes the role of American opinion in shaping both
        American and British policy in Ireland. A great deal of
        valuable   information   on   Irish-American   nationalist
        organizations is examined. A well-documented work that is
        a great source of bibliographic material on the struggle
        during the period.

180   _____. 1981. All Standards of Human Conduct: The
        American Committee on Conditions in Ireland 1920-1921.
        Eire/Ireland, 16:4:59-74.
                A discussion of an organization created to
        investigate the aggressive acts committed by the British in
        Ireland. The author fears that the testimony before the
        Committee is one of the most important of the many
        accounts of the suffering caused by the war in Ireland. He
        feels that work of the committee had a strong influence on
        public opinion at the time. But he also notes a strong
        nationalist bias among those who appeared before the
        Commission.

181   _____. 1982. The American Committee for Relief in
        Ireland 1920-1922. *Irish Historical Studies*, 23:89:30-49.
                The political and economic role of the American
        Committee for Relief in Ireland during 1920-1922, based on
        rich primary source material. It focuses on how the
        Committee was created, how effective it was in raising
        money and how the relief issue affected world politics. The

author concludes that the Committee was important and very successful, financially and politically.

182   ____. 1982. De Valera and the Americans: The Early Years 1916-1928. *Canadian Journal of Irish Studies*, 8:1:36-54.

Discusses De Valera's impact on the American public during the years 1916-1923. It deals with De Valera's slow recognition, but eventual contributions to the national cause in America as well as the controversy surrounding his beliefs and ideology. The author stresses the impact of De Valera's personality in relation to response to him.

183   ____. 1985. American and Irish Political Independence 1910-1933. In: *The Irish in American: Emigration, Assimilation and Impact*. P.J. Drudy, ed. Cambridge University, New York. pp. 271-294

An interesting overview of the American role in the Irish struggle for independence especially during the crucial period from 1914-1921. Carroll studies the propaganda battle, fund raising efforts and political pressures generated by various Irish-American groups. He also discusses De Valera's attempt to gain control of the Friends of Irish Freedom and the eventual split of the movement. Although the British government was pressured by the American government to deal with the Irish question such pressure must be viewed in a broader American context not just with reference to the problem of Irish-American pressure.

184   Clark, D. 1983. Eireannach Eigin: William J. Bradley (1892-1981) Sinn Fein Advocate. *Eire/Ireland*, 28:2:116-126.

An interesting article about William Bradley from Derry and his contributions to the Irish nationalist cause starting with his emigration to Philadelphia in 1910. Clark recounts his involvement with Clan na Gael from the lead up to 1916 on through the re-emergence of the struggle in 1969 until his death in 1981.

185   Clark, J.I.C. 1925. *My Life and Memories*. Dodd and Mead, New York.

A biography of an Irish-American journalist, editor, poet and playwright who headed the Friendly Sons of St. Patrick and the American Irish Historical Society. He was a Fenian at age 20 and left for America to avoid the British police in 1868. Though a conservative business type in the United States he supported Sinn Fein separatism and opposed anglicization.

186   Cohalan, D.F. 1919. *The Freedom of the Seas*. Friends of Irish Freedom, New York.

A pamphlet attacking Britain as an immense empire ruled by a hereditary few. He suggested that the United States and Britain were destined to come into conflict over control of the seas in order for the United States to gain commercial superiority.

187   _____. 1919. *The Indictment*. Friends of Irish Freedom, New York.

A concise statement written by Judge Daniel Cohalan that articulates the viewpoints of the Friends of Irish Freedom/Clan na Gael on the Irish question. It traces the manipulation of world opinion by Britain in order to maintain her hold on Ireland. He also marshals the reasons why America should break its emotional and political ties with England.

188   _____. 1921. Our Economic Interest in Ireland. *Forum*, 65:59-67.

An article written after World War I by Judge Daniel Cohalan on the economic reasons behind why England refused to leave Ireland. It stresses the importance to Britain of controlling the Atlantic Ocean and protecting Irish markets from foreign competition.

189   Cohalan, D.F. 1924. America's Advice to Ireland. In: *The Voice of Ireland*. W.G. Fitzgerald ed. Virtue and Company, Dublin, pp. 212-214.

A brief article by Judge Cohalan of the Clan na Gael on the economic and political repression of Ireland by Great Britain in a context of colonialism. He calls for Ireland to banish partition and pull even further away from Britain economically.

190   Cronin, S. 1972. *The McGarrity Papers: Revelations of the Irish Revolutionary Movement in Ireland and America 1900-1940*. Anvil, Tralee, County Kerry.

This study is based on the papers of Joseph McGarrity, Philadelphia businessman and a major leader of the Clan na Gael. It is an impressive compendium of primary material on the American role in the Irish freedom struggle from the turn of the century to the Second World War. The work touches on all important Irish-American issues of the time from the founding of the Clan na Gael to Wilson's crack down on the Irish and the Irish Civil War and on the bombing campaign in England at the start of World War II. It is an obligatory source for those studying the Clan na Gael, as well as, the development and substance of Irish nationalism in America.

191   _____. 1987. *Washington's Irish Policy 1916-1986: Independence, Partition, Neutrality*. Anvil Books, Dublin.

A detailed scholarly account of American foreign policy in relation to Ireland's quest for independence from 1916 to the present times. Written by an astute student of Irish nationalist history and ideology.

192   Cuddy, E. 1967. Irish-American Propagandists and American Neutrality, 1914-1917. *Mid-America*, 49:4:252-274.

A study that analyzes the post-1914 efforts of Irish-Americans to influence American foreign policy from siding with Britain in its struggle with Germany. The Irish-American press and many Irish groups attempted to reinterpret the war for Americans from a pro-German perspective. In combination with German-Americans the Irish-American propagandists divided the nation and possibly delayed entry into that conflict for two and a half years. The author found no evidence though, that the administration altered its policies under direct pressure from the Irish.

193   ____. 1968. Pro-Germanism and American Catholicism 1914-1917. *Catholic Historical Review*, 54:427-454.
An analysis of pro-German tendencies within the church largely emanating from immigrant nationalists. The author stresses the church's objectives of peace, neutrality and patriotism during wartime. The church equivocated at times but in the end demanded loyalty to the United States from her immigrant flock.

194   ____. 1969. Irish-Americans and the 1916 Elections: An Episode of Immigrant Adjustment. *American Quarterly*, 21:228-243.
A study of potential Irish-American defection from the Democrats during the election of 1916 in response to Woodrow Wilson's anti-Irish policies abroad. The author concludes from analysis of election returns that the Irish-American vote tended to be heavily pro-Wilson. It appears that Democratic policies and ideology were bread and butter issue for the Irish-Americans, in spite of Wilson's failure to side with Ireland in its struggle with Britain. However, the Catholic Church and the labor movement applied great pressure in order to keep Irish-Americans in the Democratic camp.

195   ____. 1976. Are the Bolsheviks Any Worse Than The Irish? Ethno Religious Conflict in America During the 1920's. *Eire/Ireland*, 11:3:13-32.
An interesting article that proposes that as Irish Catholic influence grew after World War I "nativists" felt threatened. The Irish-Americans were perceived as a threat to the future of the United States. The author feels that most historians have neglected the impact of Irish hyphenism on the vehement anti-Catholic reaction by nativists.

196   ____. 1981. The Irish Question and the Revival of Anti-Catholicism in the 1920's. *Catholic Historical Review*,

67:2:236-255.

A discussion of the interaction of American patriotism and Irish nationalism at the end of World War I. Many Americans felt that Irish activities before and during World War I were traitorous, and that the Catholic clergy tried to sabotage the allied war effort. The author believes that this and the fear of the increasing power of Irish Catholics lead to a revival of anti-Catholicism and anti-popery in the United States.

197   Cuddy, J.E. 1965. *Irish-America and National Isolationism: 1914-1920.* SUNY at Buffalo. Ph.D. Dissertation. (Reprinted 1976, Arno Press, New York)

A dissertation that discusses the conflict between President Woodrow Wilson and Irish-American nationalists. It analyses the role the Irish played in the defeat of Wilson's League of Nations, after they felt Wilson betrayed his own principles of self determination for oppressed peoples. However, the author stresses that conflict was not isolationism versus internationalism as some have depicted it. It was actually a struggle between the pro-British internationalism of the Wilson administration and anti-British internationalism of Irish-Americans.

198   Curran, M.P. 1906. *The Life Of Patrick A. Collins With Some of His Most Notable Addresses.* Norwood, Boston.

A biography written by a close friend, Michael P. Curran, shortly after Collins' death. It is valuable for the observations only a friend could make and the reproduction of many valuable letters.

199   Davis, T.D. 1992. *Dublin's American Policy: Irish-American Diplomatic Relations 1945-1952.* Marquette University, Ph.D. Dissertation.

This dissertation contains material on the Irish anti-partition campaign of 1948-51 in the United States.

200   Davis, T.D. 1994. The Irish Civil War and the "International Propositions" of 1922-23. *Eire/Ireland,*

29:2:92-112.

An interesting article that uses the papers of Joe McGarrity to document attempts by anti-treaty forces lead by Liam Lynch to get Clan na Gael funds to buy munitions and artillery from Germany. Davis concludes that funds were inadequate and that after Lynch's death the funds ended up with the political rather than the militant republicans. He feels that even if the mission to acquire arms had succeeded it would not have altered the ultimate course of the Irish civil war. It is a useful source for information on the activities of the Clan na Gael during the Irish civil war.

201   Devoy, J. 1948. *Devoy's Post Bag 1871-1928* 2 Vols. C.J. Fallon, Dublin.

A collection of selected letters and documents from John Devoy's personal papers from the 1870's to the Anglo-Irish War. These papers are of unique value for study of the growth and development of Irish nationalism up to partition and its American connections.

202   ____. 1969. *Recollections of an Irish Rebel.* Irish University Press, Dublin. (reprint of 1929 by Charles Young, New York)

A collection of Devoy's recollections of the Irish nationalist movement from the mid 19th to the early 20th century. An excellent source on the Irish Republican Brotherhood, Fenianism and the Clan na Gael by a major participant. Devoy portrays the essential character and philosophy of Irish nationalism from the Fenians to the Rising of 1916. It includes a critical introduction by Sean O'Luing.

203   Downing, R.F. 1924. Men, Women and Memories. In: *The Voice of Ireland.* W.G. Fitzgerald ed. Virtue and Company, Dublin. pp. 215-222.

A brief review of 30 years of Irish-American support for the Irish cause. It is an interesting source for names of activists in the Ancient Order of Hibernians and the Clan na Gael.

204   Duff, J.B. 1964. *The Politics of Revenge: Ethnic Opposition to the Peace Policies of Woodrow Wilson.* Columbia University. Ph.D. Dissertation.

An excellent study of the political impact of Irish-Americans, Italian-Americans and German-Americans on the defeat of the Versailles Treaty and the League of Nations. It shows how these three groups agreed with Wilson's Fourteen Points at the time of armistice. But their ethnic interpretations of the Wilsonian implementation of the peace process marshalled massive opposition from these three groups. This opposition contributed to the rejection of the treaty and large protest vote against the Wilsonite presidential candidate in 1920.

205   _____. 1968. The Versailles Treaty and Irish Americans. *Journal of American History*, 55:582-598.

An interesting analysis of Irish-American opposition to the Versailles Treaty which did not include Irish self-determination. It discusses the Third Irish Race Convention and American Commission for Irish Independence appeal to be included at the Paris meetings, which was refused. Also, it deals with Woodrow Wilson's pro-British attitudes and conflict with Irish-Americans over self-determination.

206   Dunne, E.F. 1924. Ireland at the Paris Peace Sessions. In: *The Voice of Ireland.* W.G. Fitzgerald ed. Virtue and Company, Dublin. Pp. 223-224

A brief commentary by the former governor of Illinois Edward Dunne on the Irish-American delegation to the Paris Peace Conference in 1919.

207   Dwyer, T.R. 1972. American Efforts to Discredit De Valera During World War II. *Eire/Ireland*, 8:2:20-33.

An interesting analysis of the plan of David Gray's, the American minister to Ireland, to discredit De Valera and the Irish government during World War II by pressing

De Valera for military bases when Gray knew they would refuse. However, it was feared that De Valera would bring up partition and reawaken a powerful Irish-American element which could endanger the Anglo-American alliance. Gray did succeed in convincing many Americans that the Irish were pro-Nazi, although Gray himself knew they were not.

208 _____. 1973. *The United States and Irish Neutrality, 1939-1945.* North Texas State University. PhD Dissertation.

A chronologically organized study of the deterioration of relations between the United States government and Ireland. It also examines the anti-Irish role of the United States minister to Ireland, David Gray, in discrediting De Valera and his government. Dwyer concludes that due to American and British propaganda De Valera was erroneously depicted as being pro-Nazi or at least uncooperative in the war against Hitler. He feels the actual benevolence of the Irish toward the Allies on even military affairs was ignored. Gray apparently did not want De Valera to disrupt Anglo-American relations after the War, since the issue of partition was still important to many Irish-Americans who viewed the Roosevelt Administration as pro-British.

209 _____. 1977. *Irish Neutrality and USA 1939-1947.* Rowan and Littlefield. Totowa, New Jersey.

A study of De Valera's efforts to maintain Irish neutrality during World War II. The author examines the views of the American press and the efforts by Roosevelt and Churchill to enlist Irish-American pressure on De Valera to join the war. It includes much materials from David Gray, the anglophile representative of the United States to Dublin. In the end, Dwyer documents how American public opinion or fear of it allowed Ireland to remain neutral.

210 Egan, P.F. 1916. What an Irishman Thinks of the Irish-German Alliance. *Forum,* 56:139-146.

A political attack on the Clan na Gael and the Irish-German alliance prior to the 1916 Rising in Ireland. A great example of blatant propaganda by a constitutional nationalist in the Redmond mold and a member of the American diplomatic corps.

211   Esslinger, D.R.   1967.   American German and Irish Attitudes Toward Neutrality, 1914-1917: A Study of Catholic Minorities. *Catholic Historical Review*, 53:194-216.

A study that in large part deals with the attitudes of German-American Catholics toward American neutrality during World War I. However, it does include some interesting considerations of the Irish Catholic position on the conflict. The author concludes that Catholics differed from other citizens on the war. He also concludes that a majority of Catholics were sympathetic toward Germany until the United States entered the war. It also includes some material on Italian- and Polish-Americans.

212   Fitzgerald, W. 1924. *The Voice of Ireland*. John Heywood Ltd., Dublin.

A wonderful collection of articles by contemporary activists in both Ireland and America on a wide variety of issues of significance to those involved in the Irish struggle. The topics range from the Gaelic psyche to the role of women to the role of DeValera in splitting the Irish-American nationalist movement. A rich source of both the popular and the academic feelings of those who lived through the final phases of the pre-partition struggle.

213   Flannigan, J.H.Jr. 1962. *United States Senator David I. Walsh and the League of Nations Issue 1918-1920*. University of Detroit. Masters Thesis.

An interesting discussion of David I. Walsh the first democratic Senator from Massachusetts since the Civil War, and his part in the congressional fight against approval of the League of Nations. The author shows that Walsh's opposition to the treaty was not due to simple hatred of English as some scholars have reported. Flannigan uncovers the development of Walsh's views from support for Woodrow Wilson's policies to vigorous opposition to Wilson's dream, the League of Nations. However, his opposition to Wilson is presented as being well reasoned, respectful, and in tune with the wishes of the vast majority of his constituents.

214   Freeman, J.B. 1983. Catholics, Communists, and Republicans: Irish Workers and the Organization of the Transport Workers Union. In: *Working Class America.* M.H. Frisch and D.J. Walkowitz, eds. University of Illinois, Urbana. Pp.256-283.

A well documented account about Irish participation in the Transport Workers Union of America (TWU) and the interactions of Irish Republicans and communists in the Union. The article is primarily about Union organizing and ideology, but it includes material on Clan na Gael connection with the Union and former members of the Irish Republican Army (IRA) who were leaders in the Union.

215   Gaffney, T. St. John. 1931. *Breaking the Silence: England, Ireland, Wilson and the War.* Liveright, New York.

A book by the former American consul at Dresden who was forced to resign in October 1915, by President Wilson. The author attempts to present from his diplomatic experience an alternative explanation of the nature of the war between Britain and the Germany. He also recounts his efforts to promote the cause of Irish freedom in Germany and his collaboration with the Irish rebel leader Sir Roger Casement.

216   Gaolbraith, J.S. 1947. United States and Ireland, 1916-1920. *South Atlantic Quarterly*, 46:192-203.

An interesting narrative that discusses the strength and significance of the Irish American vote from the Easter Rising of 1916 to the founding of the Irish Free State. A strong emphasis on the conflict between Irish Americans and Woodrow Wilson.

217   ____. 1949. United States, Britain and the Creation of the
Irish Free State. *South Atlantic Quarterly*, 48:566-574.
           A brief discussion of the treaty negotiations for the
formation of an Irish Free State in light of the necessity for
strong Anglo-American co-operation in world affairs.

218   Garner, S. 1967. Some Notes on Harold Frederick in
Ireland. *American Literature*, 39:1:60-74.
           A study of an American journalist and novelist who
used Irish settings for his writings. It considers his
involvement in the Home Rule movement and his disinterest
after the Parnell/Healy split in Irish Parliamentary Party.

219   Greene, T.R. 1987. Shane Leslie and Ireland (1916-1987):
England's Little Irish Organ in New York. *Eire/Ireland*,
22:4:47-71.
           The story of the anglophile associate editor of
Ireland, the journal funded by the Irish Parliamentary Party
of John Redmond. The journal was opposed by Clan na
Gael and the Friends of Irish Freedom because it defended
Redmond's politics to the American public. It is a study that
highlights the ambiguity and crises of loyalty probably
experienced by many in the Anglo-Irish world.

220   Hachey, T.E. 1968. The Irish Question: The British Foreign
Office and the American Political Convention of 1920.
Eire/Ireland, 3:3:92-106.
           In 1960 public access to British Foreign Office
papers, up to and including 1922, allowed Hachey to
investigate the attitudes, procedures, and responses to
American involvement in the Irish question. He found that
the British chose to play a low-key role rather than be drawn
into a public debate with Irish-Americans. However, they
kept a watchful eye on the situation.

221   ____. 1975. British War Propaganda and the American
Catholics, 1918. *Catholic Historical Review*, 61:48-66.
           A short note based on British Foreign Office papers

in which Hachey presents a series of Foreign Office memos that give clues to British planning and strategy to try and get the United States involved in World War I. The British felt that it was imperative that they limit or neutralize the political power of not only Irish American Catholics, but other ethnic American Catholics as well.

222   _____. 1976. Irish America and the Cause of Ireland at the 1919 Paris Peace Conference. In: *Varieties of Irish America, Varieties of Ireland*. B.M. Touhill, edt. University of Missouri, St. Louis. pp.211-218.

    A brief consideration of Irish American attempts to allow Ireland to be represented at the Paris Peace Conference of 1919, in order to plead its case for self-determination.

223   Hackett, F. 1914. Where the Irish Radical Stands. *New Republic*, 1:16-18.

    A pre-World War I piece in a popular American political periodical that discusses the Irish position on where the Irish will stand if the British Empire goes to war. The author felt support should be contingent on a guarantee of home rule for Ireland.

224   _____. 1916. A Policy for Ireland. *New Republic*, 6:209-211.

    A Pre-World War I commentary which was apparently a reaction of this journalist to the March 1916 Irish Race Convention in New York City. While condemning Britain for Ireland's oppressed position, the author chides most of the speakers, with a few exceptions, as at best ballroom revolutionaries. He calls for a more substantive commitment from Irish American separatists than the talk he heard at the Convention.

225   Jacobson, M.F. 1992. *Special Sorrows: Irish-, Polish- and Yiddish-Americans Nationalism and the Diasporic Imagination*. Brown University, Ph.D. Dissertation.

    A study of the genesis and development of three ethnic nationalisms at the turn of the century. It compares political liberation organizations, journalism, secular festivities and popular culture in the three groups. The author feels that nationalist thought was pervasive in immigrant life. He challenges theories that deny the reality of strong attachments to homeland politics. An epilogue is needed that attempts to examine the 20th century legacy of nationalism and its effects on even third and fourth generation ethnics.

226   Jamison, A. 1942. *Irish America, the Irish Question and American Diplomacy 1845-1921*. Harvard University, Ph.D. Dissertation.

An early study of the effects of Irish-American political pressure related to Irish independence on American diplomacy. A major conclusion of Jamison is that Irish and German opposition to Woodrow Wilson in the 1916 election had no appreciable effect on the election.

227   Jeffreys-Jones, R. 1975. Massachusetts Labor and the League of Nations Controversy in 1919. *Irish Historical Studies*, 19:76:396-416.

A detailed analysis of the defeat of the League of Nations which has been often attributed to the Irish-Americans. The author using Massachusetts, an Irish stronghold, as a test case feels that the Irish and other ethnic groups were insufficient to defeat the League alone. She feels that peace, prosperity and labor apathy were more significant.

228   Kennedy, A. 1948. *American Orator: Bourke Cockran His Life and Politics*. Bruce Humphries, Boston.

A biography of a notable Irish-American lawyer, statesman, and orator by a person who knew him well. It includes a considerable amount of material on Cockran's involvement in the struggle for Irish independence. There are several chapters that deal with the Home Rule issue, the Easter Rebellion and the controversy after World War I over Ireland's independence and the peace treaty.

229   Larkin, J. 1947. *Ireland and the Irish in the USA*. Transport
        Workers Union of America, CIO, New York.
             A pamphlet based on a speech delivered by James
        Larkin, T.D. at Manhattan Center, New York as part of the
        31st memorial commemoration of the execution of James
        Connolly. It relates the historical struggle of the Irish people
        for independence to the struggle of labor in the United
        States.

230   Leary, W.M. 1967. Woodrow Wilson, Irish-America and
        the Election, 1916. *Journal of American History*, 54:57-72.
             The author discusses why Wilson was re-elected in
        1916 even though the Irish-American voting block appeared
        to be against him. He deals with the impact of Clan na
        Gael, the Irish Republican Brotherhood (IRB), and the
        Friends of Irish Freedom, as well as, the Easter Rising and
        the aftermath of the executions in Dublin. The author feels
        that Irish- Americans vote on American issues rather the
        Irish ones. The greatest influences on voting behavior were
        economic interests, the unspectacular campaign of Hughes
        and most important the fact that Wilson had kept them out
        of the War at this point.

231   Leslie, S. 1917. *The Irish Issue in its American Aspect*.
        Charles Scribners, New York.
             A regular discussion of the Irish independence issue
        from an American perspective by an author who has definite
        pro-British bias. He is obviously a cynical observer of the
        development of Irish nationalism. The author is also guilty
        of the use of a lot of stereotypes of the Irish and very
        judgmental logic cloaked in a patronizing attempt to appear
        objective.

232   McCartan, P. 1932. *With De Valera in America*. Brentano,
        New York. Fitzpatrick Press, Dublin.
             An attempt to document the activities of De Valera
        in America both success and failures in an effort to show
        massive support for Irish independence in America. It is

most useful for its detailed itinerary and some significant
appendices.

233   McGuire, J.K. 1915. *The King, the Kaiser and Irish
Freedom*. Devin-Adair, New York.
        A book by James McGuire an Irish-American
democrat and former mayor of Syracuse, New York which
attacked Redmond's policy during World War I. He felt
that Ireland's real hope for freedom lay with a German
victory not parliamentary agitation.

234   ____. 1916. *What Germany Could Do For Ireland?* Wolfe
Tone Co., New York.
        Another work by ex-mayor McGuire that extols the
virtues of German victory and its relationship to Irish
freedom. He felt the story of Catholic Belgium being
crushed by Germany was a "red herring" meant to draw
Irishmen into the fight against Germany. It was revealed in
1919, however, that McGuire received $22,000 from the
German government to finance his activities.

235   McGurrin, J. 1948. *Bourke Cockran: A Free Lance in
American Politics*. Scribner's, New York.
        A biography of a great liberal Irish-American
politician and lawyer who was an important player in the
struggle for Irish freedom.

236   McSweeney, E.F. 1919. *Ireland is an American Question*.
Friends of Irish Freedom, New York.
        A pamphlet written by a Boston lawyer and member
of the Friends of Irish Freedom. McSweeney presents the
argument that the League of Nations was an instrument for
British oppression in Ireland, as well as, Britain's attempt to
maintain domination of the seas.

237   Maloney, W.J.M.A. 1918. The Irish Issue in its
International Aspect. *America*, 20:229-233.
        Maloney suggested that the League of Nations
would be powerless against an England that maintained its

Irish bases. He further contended that a free Ireland was necessary to prevent Britain from controlling the League of Nations for her own purposes. A free Ireland was necessary for the equilibrium of the world.

238   Mason, R. 1923. *Rebel Ireland*. American Association for the Recognition of the Irish Republic, San Francisco.
       An interesting booklet on the state of the Irish Free State by an American writer of English birth.   After travelling to Ireland to observe the situation first hand, Mason finds the Free State wanting. He decided that De Valera and the republican idealists represent the moral high ground in their opposition to the British Empire and Irish Free State participation in it.   It is very poetic in its presentation and stresses the role of Ireland's distinctive Gaelic heritage in the struggle for freedom.

239   Maxwell, K.R. 1967-68. Irish Americans and the Fight for Treaty Ratification. *Public Opinion Quarterly*, 31:620-641.
       An excellent summary and analysis of the Irish-American reaction to President Wilson's refusal to make independence for Ireland an issue at the Versailles Treaty Conference. It also chronicles their participation in the rejection of the League of Nations by Congress through pressure or congressperson and coalition building with isolationists and anglophobes.   Lots of references to individuals, and organizations significant to the treaty ratification fight.

240   Mulcrone, M.P. 1993. *The World War I Censorship of the Irish-American Press*. University of Washington, Ph.D. Dissertation.
       A study of the censorship of the Irish-American press during World War I concentrating on *The Advocate, The Irish Press, The Gaelic American, The Freemans Journal* and *The Irish World*. It examines two aspects of the press; first how the immigrant press gave a voice to immigrants and helped maintain their identity and second how loyalty to Ireland produced backlash against the Irish-American press.

The author highlights the role of the mainstream press in encouraging anti-Irish sentiments. The author concludes that although censorship supposedly involved national security, it was really an expression of the debate about American identity and the limits of pluralism during wartime. This is an excellent study of the ideology and politics of a time period when the suppression of freedom of expression was at its height in American history. Its implications for today are also self-evident.

241   Noer, T.J. 1973. The American Government and the Irish Question During World War I. *South Atlantic Quarterly* 72:1:95-114.

An interesting discussion of the Clan na Gael's attempt to keep the United States out of the war, and the battle between Woodrow Wilson and the Clan for American public opinion. It also discusses Lloyd George's machinations to influence American opinion by hatching a plot between Sinn Fein and Germany.

242   O'Connell, D.T. 1924. Irish Influence on America's Foreign Policy. In: *The Voice of Ireland*. W.G. Fitzgerald ed. Virtue and Company, Dublin, pp. 236-238.

A brief article by the director of The Friends of Irish Freedom National Bureau in Washington that recounts Irish America's lobbying against the League of Nations.

243   O'Connell, W.H. 1919. Ireland: One and Undivided. In: *Sermons and Addresses of His Eminence Cardinal William O'Connell*. Volume 6:190-198, Boston.

The views of a prominent member of the hierarchy on Irish freedom as expressed in his sermons and speeches.

244   O'Doherty, K. 1957. *Assignment America: De Valera's Mission to the United States*. DeTanko, New York.

A detailed description of De Valera's visit to America from June 1919 to December 1920 in an effort to gain recognition for the Irish Republic and obtain a loan to fund the republican struggle against British forces. It attempts to present the obstacles in his way and his efforts at trying to deal with them. The visit was quite successful, in spite of active opposition from some Irish-American leaders. It is a valuable documentation of the impact of Irish-Americans on the Irish freedom struggle of 1919-1920.

245   O'Grady, J.P. 1963. *Irish-Americans, Woodrow Wilson and Self-Determinations: A Re-evaluation*. Records of American Catholic Historical Society of Philadelphia, 74:159-173.

        O'Grady examines the thesis of Tansill, that Woodrow Wilson's anti-Irish prejudice and anglophilia totally explain the failure of Ireland's case at the Versailles Peace Conference in 1919. He concludes that Wilson's prejudices played a part, but do not explain the whole story, for European politics, not Wilson's viewpoints controlled the conference.

246   O'Hare, M.J. 1959. *The Public Career of Patrick Andrew Collins*. Boston College. PhD Dissertation.

        A well documented study on a leader in the Fenian movement and Land League in the United States, who eventually became mayor of Boston. It includes extensive material on both the Fenians and Land League in Massachusetts. It traces Collins move from militant physical force nationalism to more moderate constitutional nationalism. It includes valuable analysis of the splits within the Land League that involved Collins, Patrick Egan and Patrick Ford of *The Irish World*. The appendex material is valuable as starting point for further research on individual participation in Irish American nationalist politics, since it lists the names of delegates to the second Fenian convention as well as the location of Fenian circles in Massachusetts. A very useful source on late 19th century Irish American activities in the Boston area.

247   ____. 1967. The Irish. In: *The Immigrants Influence on Wilson Peace Politics*. J.P. O'Grady edt. University of Kentucky, Lexington. pp. 56-84

        An interesting discussion of the attempt by Irish-

Americans to influence Woodrow Wilson and create political pressure for recognition of Ireland's right to independence. It includes a nice tight discussion of political maneuvering in Congress and the work of Judge Cohalan and The Friends of Irish Freedom. The author feels that in the end both Wilson and the Irish lost since Wilson lost his League and the Irish did not gain independence.

248   Parkes, J.P. 1984. America's Lonely Stance and Irish Independence 1916-1921. In: *The American Irish Revival*. K.M. Cahill, edt. Associated Faculty Press, Port Washington, New York. pp.321-328.

An interesting brief article that documents the magazine *America*'s support for Irish independence from 1916-1921. A revealing commentary on its editor Reverend Richard Tierney, S.J., which begs further investigation of his Irish nationalism.

249   Quill, M. 1944. *Justice...for Ireland*. Transport Workers Union of America, CIO, New York.

A brief pamphlet written by Mike Quill head of Transport Workers Union of America (TWUA) and former Irish Republican Army (IRA) soldier on the continued illegal partition of Ireland.

250   Raymond, R.J. 1983. American Public Opinion, and Irish Neutrality, 1939-1945. *Eire/Ireland*, 18:1:20-45.

A article that attempts to call into question Ryle Dwyer hypothesis that American public opinion protected Ireland from Britain. Raymond believed that partition protected Ireland and feels that neutrality had a negative effect on American opinion on Ireland. It includes statistical tables to support his contention, that summarize a content analysis of United States newspapers by the Office of War Information (OWI). One should be cautious of material emanating from the OWI, especially while a war is in progress. Also, given his previous track record on Irish-American topics one should carefully consider Raymond's interpretation.

251   _____. 1983. Irish-Americans and Isolationism, 1930-1944.
         In: *The Historian's Project*. G.S. Wiegal and R. Pickus, eds.,
         London.
                  The author suggests that Irish neutrality in World
         War II was a devastating blow to Irish-American
         nationalism. He feels that this, along with discrediting of the
         Irish-American isolationists weakened Irish-American
         anglophobia, although he does not present any empirical
         evidence to support such direct effects in the Irish-American
         community.

252   Reid, B.L. 1968. *The Man From New York: John Quinn and
         His Friends*. Oxford University, New York.
                  A biography of a New York politician, who was a
         Clan na Gael member and a close friend of Daniel Cohalan.
         He turned away from the Clan during World War I
         supporting American entry into the war. After the Anglo
         Irish War however, he opposed partition as a solution to the
         Irish problem. He was a great supporter of Roger Casement
         during his fund raising efforts in 1914 and fought to prevent
         Casement's execution in 1916. Finally, he fought to preserve
         Casement's reputation after his death and subsequent
         attempts by the British to smear his reputation among Irish-
         American Catholics.

253   Rosenberg, J.L. 1976. *America and the Neutrality of Ireland,
         1939-1941*. University of Iowa. Ph.D. Dissertation.
                  A study of Irish neutrality in World War II, which
         had the support of most Irish-Americans and led to the
         development for the first time of a conflict in the interests of
         Ireland and America. It is heavily based on the personal
         correspondence and diplomatic dispatches of the American
         Ministry of Dublin, David Gray a self-professed anglophile.

254   Rowland, T.J. 1992. *Irish-American Catholics and World War
         I, 1914-1917*. George Washington University, Ph.D.
         Dissertation.
                  The author attempts to demonstrate that Irish-
         American attitudes toward World War I were shaped by

political and social views that were compatible with American culture. He feels that despite considerable tension and conflict among Irish-American Catholics about their sympathies, the Catholic Church urged them to use this opportunity to show their loyalty to America. Irish issues were of peripheral importance to most Irish-American Catholics during World War I.

255   Sarbaugh, T.J. 1980. *Culture, Militancy and De Valera: Irish-American Republican Nationalism in California 1900-1936*. San Jose State University. Masters Thesis.

    An excellent study of the development of Irish-American republican nationalism in California during the years of 1900-1936. The author contends that it was the Bachelors Walk incident in 1914, not the Rising of 1916 that was a turning point for Irish-American nationalists in California. It is a detailed chronology and analysis of a wide variety of republican activity and the impact of personalities from Father Peter Yorke to Joseph Scott and Eamon De Valera. An outstanding contribution to the literature of Irish-American nationalism.

256   _____. 1981. Irish Republicanism vs. Pure Americanism: California Reaction to De Valera's Visit. *California History*, 60:2:172-185.

    A description of De Valera's 1919 trip to California which included a successful engagement in San Francisco area in the early summer of which he returned to the east with a planned return to the west. In the fall when he returned the American Legion organized opposition to his appearance in Portland, Oregon, San Francisco, and Los Angeles (led by *The Los Angeles Times*). The assault continued and culminated in a lock out of the Shrine Auditorium. A good example of the excesses of "pure Americanism" and pro-British lackeyism on the part of *The Los Angeles Times*.

257   _____. 1981. John Byrne: The Life and Times of the Forgotten Irish Republican of Los Angeles. *Southern*

California Quarterly, 63:4:374-391.

A written article on the involvement of county Wicklow immigrant John Byrne in the Friends of Irish Freedom (FOIF) and the American Association for the Recognition of the Irish Republic (AAFRIR). It details the split between the FOIF and AARIR in California. An interesting study in individual idealism and dedication to a political cause.

258   ____. 1983. British War Policies in Ireland 1914-1918: The California Irish American Reaction. *San Jose Studies*, 9:1:24-33.

A short but very interesting piece that centers around Father Peter Yorke and the Friends of Irish Freedom activities surrounding the British entry into World War I and the prospect of introducing conscription into Ireland. It also details the dispute between Yorke and Garrett W. McEnerney over Irish-American support for World War I.

259   ____. 1985. Eamon De Valera and the Irish Press in California 1928-1931. *Eire/Ireland*, 20:4:15-22.

An examination of the American Association for the Recognition of the Irish Republic's last major effort in support of De Valera. In a less than thirty day stay in the United States De Valera promoted his newspaper in Ireland *The Irish Press* and established a national organization, American Promotion Committee (APC) to raise funds for the paper. *The Irish Press* eventually became the second largest daily in Ireland and Irish-Americans played an important role in its beginning.

260   ____. 1987. American Recognition and Eamon de Valera: The Heyday of Irish Republicanism in California 1920-1922. *Southern California Quarterly*, 69:2:133-150.

A study of the American Association for Recognition of the Irish Republic attempts to mobilize pressure in United States government to recognize the Irish Republic. It details the campaign in California from 1920 to

the signing of the treaty in 1922 that established the Irish
Free State.   It also mentions the various splits in the
movement and the disillusionment of some after the
ratification of the treaty partitioning Ireland.

261   _____. 1984. Ireland of the West: The Development of Irish
           Republicanism in California 1900-1916. *Pacific Historian*,
           28:43-51.
                  A well organized introduction to the emergence in
           California of militant Irish Republicanism out of the Gaelic
           League after the Bachelors Walk incident in Ireland and the
           postponement by British Parliament of Home Rule .

262   _____. 1990. Eamon De Valera and the Northwest: Irish
           Nationalism Confronts the Red Scare. *Pacific Northwest
           Quarterly*, 81:4:145-151.
                  An interesting account of a rarely studied issue, De
           Valera's American campaign in the Pacific Northwest
           between November 7 and November 15, 1919.   After a
           powerful welcome among Irish-Americans in Butte Montana,
           he was denounced in Spokane, Seattle and Portland by the
           American Legion as a symbol of un-Americanism and a
           foreign threat. Although De Valera was caught up in a sea
           of intolerant pure Americanism and anti-communist rhetoric
           Sarbaugh recounts how he effectively dealt with the
           situations within each local context.

263   Splain, J.J. 1924. The Irish Movement in the United States
           Since 1911. In: *The Voice of Ireland*. W.G. Fitzgerald, ed.
           Virtue and Company, Dublin. Pp. 225-235.
                  An interesting history of Irish-American activism
           between 1911 and 1919 by John Splain, Vice-President of
           The Friends of Irish Freedom. He describes the activities of
           the Irish Race Conventions, the Irish American delegation
           to the Paris Peace Conference and Irish-American pressures
           on the United States Congress. This piece is a valuable
           source of names of Irish-American activists from across the
           country.

264   _____. 1924. Under Which King? In: *The Voice of Ireland.*
           W.G. Fitzgerald, ed. Virtue and Company, Dublin. pp. 242-
           254.
                   A lengthy discussion by John Splain, Vice-President
           of the Friends of Irish Freedom, on Eamon de Valera's
           errors in the United States. He documents the division of
           the Irish movement into the Friends of Irish Freedom and
           the American Association for the Recognition of the Irish
           Republic. A good source for the basis of popular animosity
           towards De Valera among many Irish-American activists by
           a person who was a participant.

265   Sullivan E.M. 1984. Eamon De Valera and the Forces of
           Opposition in America 1901-1920. *Eire/Ireland*, 19:2:99-115.
                   An interesting study of struggle between Eamon De
           Valera and his American supporters Patrick McCarten and
           Joseph McGarrity and his American opponents Daniel
           Cohalan and John Devoy over control of Irish-American
           nationalism. The De Valera group which did not oppose the
           existence of a League of Nations if Ireland were an
           independent participant thought that Cohalan was diverting
           attention from the fight for Irish freedom to opposition to
           the League. It also includes a discussion of the maneuvering
           of the British ambassador, as well as how the factionalism
           among Irish-American groups hindered American political
           recognition of the Irish Republic.

266   Sullivan, M.J. 1968. *Hyphenism in St. Louis, 1900-1921:
           The View From the Outside.* St. Louis University. Ph.D.
           Dissertation.
                   This study includes an extensive chapter on Irish-
           American nationalism in St. Louis at the turn of the century.
           It is part of a larger study on hyphenism in time and place.

           It is an excellent source of primary material on Irish
           nationalism in the midwest.

267   _____. 1971. Fighting for Irish Freedom: St. Louis Irish-
           Americans, 1918-1922. *Missouri Historical Society*, 65:184-

206.
A history of the founding and subsequent activities
of the Friends of Irish Freedom in St. Louis during the
Anglo-Irish War and up to the Irish Civil War. It includes
a thorough discussion with the League of Nations conflict in
the St. Louis area, as well as the decline of Irish-American
nationalist groups in St. Louis after the Irish Civil War.

268   ____. 1972. Constitutionalism, Revolution and Culture,
Irish-American Nationalism in St. Louis, 1920-1914. *Missouri
Historical Society Bulletin*, 28:4:234-245.
A discussion of how Irish-American nationalism
differed from the national law that constitutionalism had
triumphed over revolutionism.   Sullivan shows how
nationalists in St. Louis diffused into cultural, constitutional
and revolutionary elements. In St. Louis revolutionary
nationalism had deeper roots than constitutional nationalism
but the struggle between these two forces became bitter and
very divisive.

269   ____. 1976. The Irish in St. Louis: The Role of
Nationalism in the Irish-American Community. In: *Varieties
of Ireland, Varieties of Irish America*. B.M. Touhill, edt.
University of Missouri, St. Louis. Pp.31-40.
A very brief, well-written introduction to the
development of Irish-American nationalism in a small
midwestern city.

270   Tansill, C.C. 1957. *America and the Fight for Irish Freedom,
1886-1922*. Devin-Adair, New York.
A comprehensive study of Irish-American
nationalism until 1922 by a sympathetic scholar who was the
grandson of a Fenian. It also includes a introductory chapter
covering the period 1801-1881. All major groups, individuals
and controversies are covered in this detailed heavily
documented work. It has been criticized by some as having
some errors in facts, but the overall story and analysis is
dead on.   This work is an essential starting point for
research and reading in this area scholastically.

271   Tarpey, M.V. 1969. *The Role of Joseph McGarrity in the Struggle for Irish Independence.* St. Louis University. Ph.D. Dissertation. (Reprinted 1976, Arno Press, New York).

A massive, well-documented study of the role of Joseph McGarrity in the struggle for Irish freedom. It is a significant study of a physical force republican who had no patience with gradualists. It is an important source of material on the Clan na Gael. McGarrity never wavered from the ideal of a 32 county republic and spent 47 years and two personal fortunes pursuing that ideal.

272   _____. 1971. Joseph McGarrity, Fighter for Irish Freedom. *Studia Hibernica,* 11:164-180.

A brief well-written history of the growth and development of Joseph McGarrity's dual republicanism. It is a sympathetic, humane account of a man who devoted his life to the principles of Wolfe Tone and Robert Emmet, both in Ireland and in America as leader of Clan na Gael.

273   Tucker, D.M. 1967. Some American Responses to the Easter Rebellion, 1916. *Historian,* 29:605-618.

An interesting discussion of the response of the American press to the 1916 Easter Rebellion. The author briefly examines the editorial position of anglophile media like *The New York Times; The Wall Street Journal and The North America Review,* and the liberals like *The Cleveland Pain Dealer, New Republic and The Nation.* He also relates changes in editorial stance related to the public executions of the leaders of the Rising.

274   Walsh, J.P. 1962. De Valera in the United States, 1919. *Records of the American Catholic Historical Society of Philadelphia,* 73:3-4:92-107.

A brief chronology and narrative description of De Valera's speaking tour of the United States in 1919 and especially the reactions of the media to his message.

275   _____. 1967. Woodrow Wilson Historians vs. the Irish. *Eire/Ireland,* 2:2:55-66.

A brief discussion of the attempt of an Irish-American delegation to represent Ireland at the Paris Peace Conference after World War I. The delegates were: Frank Walsh, Dunne and Michael J. Ryan. It is based on the published diary of Lt. Colonel Stephen Bonsal, *Unfinished Business*.

276   -----. 1988. Terminal Interviews: Arthur Griffith, Michael Collins and James Duval Phelan of San Francisco. *Eire/Ireland*, 23:4:81-90.

A brief analysis of former senator James Phelan interviews with Michael Collins and Arthur Griffith during the Irish Civil War and Phelan's efforts to promote the Irish Free State point of view in America.

277   Walsh, J.P. and T.P. Foley. 1974. Father Peter C. Yorke Irish American Leader. *Studia Hibernica*, 14:90-103.

A discussion of a famous activist priest involvement in the republican movement. It also deals with Yorke's political attacks on Garrett McEnerney, James Phelan and the American Protective Association (APA).

278   Walsh, J.C. 1919. *The Invisible Irish*. Friends of Irish Freedom. New York.

A pamphlet describing efforts to bring the Irish delegation before the Paris Peace Conference.

279   Ward, A.J. 1968. America and the Irish Problem, 1899-1921. *Irish Historical Studies*, 16:61:64-90.

A well-written article that discusses Irish-American activity in behalf of Irish freedom from the Boer War to forming of the Free State. It is a valuable source of data and interpretation on the Clan na Gael and its front The Friends of Irish Freedom, as well as, the United Irish League of America. It has excellent documentation.

280   _____. 1969. *Ireland and Anglo-American Relations, 1899-1921*. University of Toronto, Toronto.

A history of Anglo-Irish relations from the Boer

War to the founding of the Irish Free State. The author attempts to reconstruct the interaction of Irish, British and American politics during this crucial period in Irish history. It is an interesting study of immigrant pressure and its impact on foreign policy. On the whole it is an objective factual study with some minor fluctuations with Tory revisionist ideas.

281   Yorke, P.C. 1918. *America and Ireland*. Friends of Irish Freedom, New York.
        A brief pamphlet put out by the Friends of Irish Freedom and written by Father Peter Yorke, the long time radical Irish-American priest activist. It was an answer to Garret McEnerney's attack on American supporters of Sinn Fein as treasonous and disloyal. Yorke insisted the Irish right to self-determination was more important than Britain's capitalist war with Germany. He personally attacked the rationality of McEnerney's arguments and for all intents and purposes ended the debate.

282   Zacharewicz, M. 1956,1957. The Attitude of the Catholic Press Toward the League of Nations. *Records of the American Catholic Historical Society of Philadelphia*, 67:3-30; 67:88-104; 68:46-50.
        A series of articles that analyze the role of the Catholic press in the battle over the League of Nations which conclude that the Catholic press was strongly in favor of the League of Nations.

CHAPTER 4

FROM CIVIL RIGHTS TO WAR OF LIBERATION:
1960'S TO TODAY

283   Alexander, S. 1982. The Patriot Game. *New York Magazine*, Nov. 22, 1982: 58-68.
        A lengthy article by a noted journalist on the trial of the IRA Five, Flannery, Falvey, Harrison, Gormley and Mullin on charges of gun running. Alexander discusses the course of the trial, the defense strategy and finally the acquittal of the Irish-American activists.

284   Barker, G. 1975. Aims For Ulster: The Irish American File. *The Spectator*, 689: (Nov 29).
        A brief article on the supply of weapons to the IRA supposedly from America as well as a commentary on Irish-American attitudes toward Britain's role in Ireland.

285   Barron, J. 1991. Breaking the IRA's American Connection. *Reader's Digest*, March 1991: 65-71.
        A highly emotional and biased account of the arrest and conviction of Richard Johnson, Christina Reed, Martin Quigley and Gerald Hay for developing weapons systems for the IRA.

286   Bond, J.C. 1982. Northern Ireland Black Eyes. *Freedomways*, 22:1:13-20.
        A brief comparison of the present day struggle in the 6 counties to that of African-Americans by the editor of *Freedomways* magazine. Her observations are based on the findings of a delegation of Black activists to northeast Ireland in the wake of 1981 hunger strikes.

287   Boyer, S. 1987. American Connection. *An Gael*, 4:1:15-17.
        A brief interview with Jack Holland, author of *The American Connection: U.S., Guns, Money and Influence in Northern Ireland*. It contains some interesting ideological hints and suggestions.

288   Bradley, J. 1993. The Greening of America. In: *The Irish Echo*, December 15-21:22-23,40. December 22-28:18-19,32.
        A lengthy two part newspaper article that appeared in New York's *Irish Echo* on the attempt by Irish-American lobbyists to make northeast Ireland a priority for the United States government. It is a broad overview of the various Irish-American groups, large and small, and their efforts in behalf of the struggle in northeast Ireland. It also covers the efforts and obstacles facing members of Congress who actively pursue a real solution to the situation in northeast Ireland.

289   Burke, M. 1981. *A Decade of Deceit: A Detailed Look at the New York Times and the War in Ireland*. Irish Northern Aid, New York.
        An interesting analysis of *The New York Times* coverage of the struggle in northeast Ireland from the birth of the provisionals to the hunger strikes. It points out many examples of anti-Irish bias as well as factual errors in the coverage of the situation. The author concludes that during the time period the *Times* has consistently misrepresented the facts and promoted a pro British point of view. A good example of Irish-American activists trying to counteract media bias.

290   Cahill, K.M. 1979-80. Healing Hands. *Foreign Policy*, 37:87-100.
        A proposal by a liberal Irish-American medical doctor that calls for a moderate American initiative largely couched in economic aid to end the impasse in northeast Ireland. Time has proved such proposals naive and impractical.

291   Cahill, K.M. and H.L. Carey. 1984. Americas Role in
        Northern Ireland. In: *The American Irish Revival*. K.M.
        Cahill ed. Associated Universities Press. Rutherford, New
        Jersey. pp. 560-567.
                A call for British withdrawal from Ireland by a pair
        of Irish-American liberals who have consistently criticized
        Irish republicanism.

292   Carey, H.C. 1984. The Politics of Death. In: *The
        American Irish Revival*. K.M. Cahill ed. Associated
        Universities Press. Rutherford, New Jersey. pp. 547-559.
                A naive, somewhat hypocritical address given in
        Ireland by the former governor of New York in which he
        pledges to oppose the support of violence in northeast
        Ireland by Irish-Americans.

293   Clark, Dennis I. 1977. *Irish Blood: Northern Ireland and
        the American Conscience*. Kennikat Press, Port Washington,
        New York.
                A brief monograph by an incisive Irish-American
        academic examining the revival of American interest in
        northeast Ireland during the beginning of the Civil Rights
        Movement. It contains excerpts of interviews with Irish-
        American activists in the early 1970's examining their
        motivation for involvement in the Irish nationalist cause.

294   Connolly, R.E. 1985. The American Role in the Conflict.
        In: *Armalite and Ballot Box*. R.E. Connolly. Cuchullain
        Publications, Fort Wayne, Indiana. Pp. 81-99.
                A brief discussion of the Irish-American role in the
        conflict in northeast Ireland by an Irish-American lawyer
        from the midwest. The book is an interesting introduction to
        the conflict especially for the uninitiated.

295   _____. 1988. *The Connolly Report*. Cuchullain Publications,
        Fort Wayne, Indiana.
                An attempt by the author, an American lawyer, to
        examine some special aspects of the British role in NE
        Ireland and the American response to such issues as the

supergrasses, extradition and the MacBride principles. It is
based to some degree on the author's personal experiences
and observations in northeast Ireland.

296   ____. 1990. *A Time to Mend: An Irish-American
Republican Solution. Cuchullain, Fort Wayne.
             This is the third work in a trilogy on Irish-American
republicanism authored by an Irish-American lawyer.
Connolly explores Ireland's economic history as a cause of
the present struggle. He calls for economic solutions and
feels that Ireland united has potential for prosperity in the
high technology of the future. Some in Ireland would
disagree with his economic solutions but his ideas certainly
merit consideration.

297   Cooke, T.C. 1984. The Quest for Peace in the North of
Ireland. In: *The American Irish Revival*. K.M. Cahill, ed.
Associated Faculty Press, Port Washington, New York. Pp.
521-529.
             A brief article by the former Cardinal of New York,
it is a plea for peaceful resolution to the struggle in the six
counties. However, it clearly outlines the British role in
creating an environment characterized by state violence,
discrimination and lack of social justice.

298   Cox, T.J. 1993. *The Trial of the IRA Five*. Riverside Books,
Ormond Beach, Florida.
             Tells the story of the trial of Mike Flannery, George
Harrison, Daniel Gormley, Thomas Falvey and Patrick
Mullen on charges of shipping machine guns and
ammunition to the IRA. It relies almost totally on trial
transcripts and presents little analysis or contextual data.
However, it does record the flow of the trial and the brilliant
defense in an interesting manner.

299   Crick, B. 1979. The Pale Green Internationalists. *The New
Statesman*, 96:888-896. (Dec. 7, 1979)
             A journalistic discussion of the Irish-American
dimension on the politics of northeast Ireland during the

Jimmy Carter administration. Carter is characterized as weak, not really at odds with British policy. But he did try to pressure both sides. The Carter administration relied heavily on American style legislative solutions and dismissed the role of the IRA in politics.

300   Cronin, S. 1987. *Washington's Irish Policy 1916-1986: Independence, Partition, Neutrality.* Anvil Books, Dublin.

A detailed scholarly account of American foreign policy in relation to Ireland's quest for independence from 1916 to the present times. Written by an astute student of Irish nationalist history and ideology.

301   Davidson, S. 1970. Bernadette Devlin: An Irish Revolutionary in Irish America. *Harper's Magazine*, 240:78-87.

A detailed itinerary of Bernadette's speaking tour of the United States from August 22 to September 2, 1969. It documents the progress and problems she encountered on the Irish-American circuit as well as her introduction to Irish-American politics. An interesting documentation of the early days of Irish-American reinvolvement in Ireland. Bernadette Devlin was the youngest person ever elected to British Parliament and one of the major spokespersons for the Northern Irish Civil Rights Association.

302   Deacy, J. 1972. The IRA, New York Brigade. *New York*, 5:11:40-44.

A popular piece written shortly after Bloody Sunday describing the Irish-American community in New York's reaction to the reemergence of the Irish issue. A brief account of the founding of Irish Northern Aid as well as the IRA split into the provos and officials.

303   Editors/The Economist. 1985. Noraid Dancing on a Gun Butt. *The Economist*, 294:7381:35-36 (Feb 16, 1985).

A very brief commentary in the *Economist* on the occasion of Thatcher's visit to Washington in Feb 1986. Irish-American groups led by Noraid called for a massive demonstration against British policies in Ireland. However, its main aim was to attack Noraid's fund raising in the U.S. and highlight the U.S. Justice Department's attempts to ban Noraid.

304   English, T. 1987. Americans in the North. *Irish America*, 3:10:16-21.
       An account of the 1987 Irish People educational trip to northeast Ireland. English does a real hatchet job on most of the participants. His account of what happened on the trip is slanted, inaccurate and apparently designed to demean or belittle their efforts. English ignores most of the heavy political activity that transpired in favor of playing up some of the social activities of a few participants.

305   Farrelly, P. 1990. An Upheaval at Noraid. *Irish America*, 6:20-22, 34-36.
       A discussion of the split that occurred in the Irish Northern Aid Committee over the issue of Sinn Fein's abandonment of abstentionism in Ireland. It emphasizes the changes in the personnel that run the organization.

306   Finn, P. 1989. Reagan, Ireland and What Happened to the Irish-American Agenda. *Irish America*, 5:1:18-21, 45.
       An examination of Reagan's non-Irish unity policy and reasons why Irish-Americans have their political clout.

307   Fisher, D. 1977. Exporting Death to Ireland. *Commonwealth*, 104:356-358. (June 10)
       A propaganda piece out of Dublin that attacks Irish-Americans for allegedly supplying guns to the IRA. It includes the usual attack on Noraid and references to Irish-American romanticism.

308   Fitzpatrick, J. 1973. The Irish American and Sinn Fein. *Triumph*, 8:13-16.
       An interesting discussion of provisional Sinn Fein and its *Eire Nua* booklet as well as its ideology and solutions to the problem of a divided Ireland. He chastises Irish-

Americans who have not built a mass movement to pressure British withdrawal. It is written by an American conservative who feels that if he lived in Ireland he would support Sinn Fein.

309   Flynn, R.L. and B.A. Morrison. 1993. *Irish-Americans For Clinton/Gore: Five Recommendations on Irish Issues.* IAFC/G, Washington D.C.
         A pamphlet prepared for the 1994 election campaign that outlines five recommendations on Irish issues for a potential Clinton/Gore administration. The five issues are: 1. Special Envoy to Northern Ireland, 2. Misuse and Abuse of the American Justice System, 3. Human Rights in Northern Ireland, 4. Immigration Standards for the Irish, 5. The MacBride Principles and Economic Investment.

310   Forster, F.J. 1989. *Undue Process.* Forbach, San Francisco.
         A personal account of harassment of an Irish-American activist by the American government. A disturbing documentation of an attempt to destroy a person professionally because of his political beliefs. A short, chilling account of the perversion of our American system of justice.

311   Golway, T. 1988. The Cardinal's Crusade. *Irish America*, 4:9:18-21.
         A brief descriptive itinerary of Cardinal O'Connor's peace pilgrimage to Ireland in the summer of 1988.

312   Greer, H. 1983. The Boys of the I.R.A. *American Spectator*, November 16, 32-34.
         A very brief diatribe about the nature and goals of the provisional IRA. The author also complains about the ignorance of Noraid members and their contribution to violence in Ireland. The tone and language of the piece is definitely pro-loyalist and anti-Irish nationalist.

313   Guelke, A. 1984. *The American Connection to the Northern Ireland Conflict.* Irish Studies in International Affairs. 1:27-

39.

An interesting academic study that traces the ups and downs of American involvement in northeast Ireland from 1979-1983. He feels it is difficult to assess the impact of American pressure, but suggests it has been erratic and unpredictable. The author also thinks that the British government is intent on preventing the American factor from fully developing.

314   Hachey, T.E. 1989. Irish-America and the Contemporary Conflict in Ireland. In: *The Irish Experience*. Hachey, T.E., J.M. Hernon and L.J. McCaffrey. Prentice Hall, Englewood Cliffs, N.J. Pp. 248-254.

An attempt to discuss Irish republicanism among Irish-Americans in the past and present. Hachey begins with a descent review of earlier involvement and presents all the simplistic theories to explain such participation. However, like so many of today's academics who quite competently deal with the "good old" Irish republicanism of the past, Hachey takes leave of his objectivity when dealing with today. The section Irish republicanism today can only be describe as a diatribe full of distortions, myths, outright falsehood, and reliance on discredited works like those of Maria McGuire and Clare Sterling.

315   Hamill, P. 1972. Notes on the New Irish: A Guide for the Goyim. *New York*, 5:11:33-39.

An interesting popular piece by a native New Yorker on how events in the six counties were responsible for the reawakening and reorganization of Irish-Americans in New York. A popular culture piece on a topic that cries for further study.

316   Hamill, P. 1994. The Irish Diaspora and the North. *Irish America*, Nov/Dec. 94.:2-26, 83.

An interesting piece by an Irish-American journalist who does have a good working knowledge of the northern situation. Hamill presents a personal perspective on the relationship of the American Irish to the struggle in the north. It is somewhat clouded by Hamill's liberal biases about the Catholic Church's ideological impact on the struggle as well as the nature of anti-government violence.

317   Healy, J.B. 1989. *The Northern Ireland Dilemma: An Irish American Imperative*. Peter Lang, New York.
       A highly structured but faulty analysis of the role of Irish-Americans in the struggle in northeast Ireland. The work has many errors of fact and interpretations. It is an anti-Irish republican work that minimizes the British role in the ongoing struggle. It is written by a business professor with a poor grasp of the dynamics of the daily struggle. However, some of his suggestions on business and organizational strategies merit further consideration.

318   Hickey, N. 1981. The Battle for Northern Ireland. *TV Guide*, 29:29:8-28. (9/26/83).
       An analytical popular article that attempts to understand the 1981 hunger strikes and their impact in sociohistorical context. A surprising change of pace for the American press coverage of the struggle in the six counties.

319   Holland, J. 1987. *The American Connection: U.S. Guns, Money and Influence in Northern Ireland*. Viking, New York.
       An attempt by a left wing liberal Irish newsman to examine the American wing of Irish republicanism. His chapters on the courts and media are good but his analysis of Irish-American organizations is weak. Holland's personal ideology permeates his interpretations and contradictions abound from one section of the work to another. However, his section on radical Irish-American activist George Harrison is especially good.

320   Holland, M. 1979. Kennedy's New Irish Policy. *The New Statesman*, May 11, 678-79.
       A brief but interesting commentary by a noted Irish journalist on Ted Kennedy's more recent attempts to blame Britain for the stalemate in Ireland instead of just condemning the IRA.

321   Hosenball, M. 1982. Irish Burlesque. *The New Republic*,
        March 3, 1982: 11-12.
                A cynical, racist piece on the struggle in northeast
        Ireland characterized by mockery of both Irish nationalists
        and loyalists while excluding any real blame on the part of
        Britain.

322   Hurley, M.J. 1990. *Blood on The Shamrock: An American
        Ponders Northern Ireland 1968-1990*. Peter Lang, New York.
                An examination of the situation in northeast Ireland
        from partition to the present by a liberal American bishop.
        It is a well documented work sympathetic to Irish
        nationalism. But Hurley's narrow opposition to the IRA and
        Sinn Fein prevents him from articulating the republican view
        point and its possible contribution to a solution.

323   Hurley, M.J. 1994. Ireland: The Stirring of the Waters.
        America. June 4, 1994: 14-16.
                A very brief commentary by an Irish-American
        bishop on the Downing Street Declaration of December
        1993 and its possible ramifications for a peace process in the
        north of Ireland.

324   Kolb, R. 1983. Unmasking the IRA: The Propaganda War
        in America. *Conservative Digest*, 9:32-33. (Feb)
                An article that attempts to tie the IRA to the PLO
        and Soviet Union. It quotes unreliable sources such as
        Maria McGuire, Yonah Alexander and Paul Wilkinson. The
        author repeats all the propaganda myths about the struggle
        and accuses the IRA of trying to promote a civil war. He
        finishes with an attack on Noraid including totally false
        statements about where the funds go. It also promotes the
        myth of the romantic Irish-American activist. This is an
        extreme piece of pro-British propaganda.

325   Kennedy, E.M. 1973. Ulster As An International Issue.
        Foreign Policy, 11:57-71.
                An early statement by an influential Irish-American
        congressperson calling for British withdrawal from Ireland.

It includes material on internment, Bloody Sunday, the abolition of Stormont and the unification of Ireland. It compares northeast Ireland to the Vietnam situation. Kennedy was severely criticized and viciously attacked in the American media for such views, possibly leading him to back off on the issue since that time.

326   Kennedy, M. 1987. A Rebel at Heart. *An Gael*, 4:1:19-22.
        A critical review of Jack Holland's book on Irish American connections to northeast Ireland by a lawyer who successfully defended the Brooklyn IRA Five. Kennedy presents a structural analysis of the book and an interesting commentary on Holland's interpretations.

327   Kyle, K. 1979. America's Ireland. *The Listener*, 101:238-239.
        A brief piece which was a reaction to a Jack Anderson column on northeast Ireland in October 1980, that exposed aspects of British prison policies in northeast Ireland. Most of the article is a attack on Noraid and Father Sean McManus of the Irish National Caucus as well as the Ad Hoc Committee on Ireland in the US Congress.

328   McCarthy, J. 1993. *Dissent From Irish America*. University Press of America, Lanham Maryland.
        A compilation by the author of his news columns on the struggle in Ireland that were largely published in *Boston Irish News*. He covers a wide variety of topics from the hunger strikes to the MacBride Principles. McCarthy is a well known apologist for the British presence in Ireland. His articles written in a journalistic style are characterized by sweeping generalizations, misinterpretations of the facts and a denigrating attitude towards those who disagree with him. However, the collection is useful since it is a great example of Tory revisionism and lackeyism at work in America. For all of his criticisms of Irish-Americans as naive, simplistic and romantic, McCarthy's work highlights his own naivete and ignorance of the situation in northeast Ireland.

329   McCarthy, J. 1987. Irish American Catholic Conservatives
        and Northern Ireland. *Records of American Catholic History
        Society of Philadelphia*, 98:69-79.
            A study based on a conservative Catholic monthly
        journal, *Triumph*, and their reporting on the happenings in
        northeast Ireland. The journal was founded in 1966 but is
        no longer in publication. The author calls attention to an
        interesting subject but interjects his own virulent anti-Irish
        republicanism into his naive slanted analysis. But the
        question does beg further, more objective analysis.

330   McDonnell, T.P. 1974. Catholic Press Reporting on
        Northern Ireland. *Holy Cross Quarterly*, 6:1-4:68-71.
            A brief study from the early 1970's that discusses the
        failure of the Catholic Press to report the real story of the
        struggle in northeast Ireland. The author feels that the
        reporting that does occur is bland and unreliable.

331   McKinley, M. 1987. Lavish Generosity: The American
        Dimension of International Support for the Provisional Irish
        Republican Army, 1968-1983. *Conflict Quarterly*, 7:2:20-42.
            An interesting but biased and naive attempt to
        analyze the American dimension of financial support for the
        Irish Republican Army between 1968-1983. An attempt to
        directly link Noraid to the IRA through funding and arms
        trafficking appears to be fundamental to this paper. The
        paper is laced with innuendos, and inaccuracies that can lead
        to false connections and conclusions.

332   McKittrick, D. 1979. The Irish Connection: Northern
        Ireland and a Powerful U.S. Minority. *Atlas World Press
        Review*, November 1979: 25-26, 28.
            A brief analysis of lobbying efforts in the U.S. by
        the Ad Hoc Committee, the Irish National Caucus and the
        "Four Horsemen" by an Irish journalist. Useful to gain an
        outsider's view of American political maneuvering.

333   McManus, S. 1993. *The MacBride Principle: Genesis and
        History and the Story To Date*. Irish National Caucus,

Washington, D.C.

A brief history of the origin and development of the MacBride Principles from the point of view of a priest lobbyist who operates out of Washington D.C. An interesting compilation of material related to raising fair employment issues in northeast Ireland here in the United States.

334   Metress, S.P. 1984. *The Hunger Strike and the Final Struggle*. Connolly Books, Detroit, Michigan.

A popular account of the ideology, history and impact of the Irish hunger strikes from an Irish-American perspective. It also includes some folk poetry related to the 1981 hunger strikes.

335   Mount, F. 1980. The IRA and the Bar Rooms of America. *The American Spectator*, 13:14-16. (Jan)

A propaganda piece in a conservative American publication that attempts to make a case for the idea that the IRA has become a totalitarian Marxist organization. It includes hypothetical financial figures for IRA funding. An attempt to convince American supporters that the IRA is red, not green.

336   Mullins, E. 1994. The American Role in the Ceasefire. *Irish America*. Nov/Dec 94: 16-17.

A very concise summary of the impact of Irish-American lobbying in both Ireland and Washington in order to bring about a political climate that would encourage a ceasefire by the IRA.

337   Murray, Hugh T. 1975. The Green and the Red Unblending: The National Association for Irish Freedom, 1972-1975. *Journal of Ethnic Studies*, 3:2:1-21.

An excellent chronicle and discussion of the role played by the National Association for Irish Freedom during the early 70's in responding to the rapidly developing war of liberation in northeast Ireland. It also presents an interesting   case   study   of   the   collapse   of   the liberal/communist coalition as a result of personality rather then ideological conflict. A must for names and events during the post Bloody Sunday revival of Irish republicanism in the United States.

338   New Republic Editor. 1975. Friends of the IRA. *The New Republic*, 173:3-5 (Oct, 18).
         A lengthy anti-Irish republican editorial that is a showcase for all the erroneous myths and generalizations about the struggle in Ireland that are regularly perpetuated by the American media. A useful study in the effects of British propaganda on the American media. It is also a biased hysterical attempt to alienate Irish-Americans from the struggle in Ireland.

339   O'Brien, C.C. 1981. The Four Horsemen. *Harper's*, 263:14-21.
         Conor Cruise O'Brien, a leading apologist for the British presence in northeast Ireland, attacks Senators Kennedy and Moynihan, Governor Carey and Speaker Tip O'Neill for speaking out on Ireland. He outlines all the myths of how Irish-Americans don't understand the situation. He also points that American pressure for Irish unity pushes Ireland toward civil war. It is typical of the propaganda associated with Conor Cruise.

340   O'Dowd, N. 1993. The Greening of the White House. *Irish America*, 9:1:18-23.
         A brief article that discusses the attempts to shape an Irish agenda for the Clinton-Gore ticket by people such as Paul O'Dwyer, Ray Flynn and Tom Manton. An interesting glimpse at the efforts of Irish America to reassemble its once vaunted political clout.

341   O'Dowd, N. 1986. First Aid For Ireland. *Irish America*, 2:5:20-23.
         An examination of the $250,000,000 U.S. aid package to aid Ireland and its political ramifications. It considers attempts by Irish-American activists to insure

proper use of the funds in a human rights context.

342   O'Dowd, N. 1985. Behind the MacBride Principles. *Irish America*, 1:1:15-17.
        A brief synopsis of an attempt by Irish-American groups to have American employers in northeast Ireland abide by American fair hiring legislation. A good summary of MacBride's beginnings and the controversy generated.

343   O'Dwyer, P. 1979. *Counsel For the Defense: The Autobiography of Paul O'Dwyer.* Simon & Schuster, New York.
        An interesting work on the life of a prominent civil rights lawyer and Irish nationalist. It includes some brief comments on the Ft. Worth Five case involving Irish Northern Aid members from New York rumored to have bought guns in Mexico for the IRA.

344   O'Murchu, S. 1987. Illinois Weighs Up the MacBride Principles. *Irish America*, 3:12:21-24.
        A detailed report of the attempt by Irish-American activists to pass the MacBride Principles in Illinois. A nice introduction to the legislative aspect of Irish-American pressure on the six counties.

345   Quinn, F. 1987. In the Shadow of the Gunmen. *Irish America*, Jan 18-20.
        A brief article on the arrest of a number of Irish-Americans on suspected gun running charges. It concentrates on the cases of Bill Norton, Hollywood screen writer and Bill Quinn, an Irish-American who joined the IRA.

346   Raymond, R.J. 1984. The United States and Terrorism in Ireland, 1969-1981. In: *Terrorism in Ireland*. Y. Alexander and A.E. Day, eds. Croom Helm, London.
        A propaganda piece couched in scholarly format by a known apologist for the British presence in northeast Ireland. Raymond attempts to show that the provisional

IRA's ideology and campaign against British rule in Ireland goes against basic Irish-American values. He uses almost every smear tactic associated with British attempts to manipulate American perceptions of the struggle in Ireland, fromMarxism to gangsterism. A fine example of value laden, pseudo-scholarly propaganda.

347   ____. 1983. Irish-America and Northern Ireland: An End to Romanticism? *The World Today*, 39:3:106-113.

Raymond, a rather vicious apologist for British rule in Ireland, uses this propaganda piece to dismiss all Irish-American interest in the struggle in Ireland as Celtic romanticism based on a warped view of Irish history. He further accuses Irish-Americans of ignorance, blind hatred and propensity to be duped by the IRA. He also has some suggestions for the British Information Services that will help counter the provos machine. This piece in the guise of legitimate academic scholarship is merely a diatribe against republicanism laced with inaccuracies of fact and the overgeneralized value judgements of the author. One would suspect that the author was actually employed by British Information Services. But alas he does have some praise for those informed, educated Irish-Americans who agree with him presumably because of their sophistication and objectivity.

348   ____. 1983. Irish-Americans and Northern Ireland: A Postscript. *The World Today*, 39:10:407-410.

A rejoinder piece by Raymond, that serves almost as an addenda to his previous piece in *The World Today* (39:3:106-113). It was apparently motivated by the election in 1983 of Mike Flannery as St. Patrick's Day Parade Grand Marshall in New York City. Raymond tries to assure that Flannery's election meant nothing politically since he was denounced by Senators Moynihan, and Ted Kennedy, ex-governor Hugh Carey and representative Tip O'Neill. It was merely a Noraid propaganda stunt engineered by a small group of young militants. Like much of Raymond's work on the troubles today it is anti-Irish but with an almost hysterical tone.

349 ____. 1984. The United States and Terrorism in Ireland, 1969-1981. In: *Terrorism in Ireland*. Y. Alexander and A. O'Day, eds. St. Martins, New York. Pp. 32-52.

A politically motivated overview of the situation in northeast Ireland from the civil rights movement to the hunger strikes of 1981 by an academic apologist for British policy in the six counties. It is work filled with errors of interpretation, use of discredited sources and anti-republican rhetoric. He also calls for intensified government activity against republican activism in the United States. Of course it appears in larger volume edited by Alexander and O'Day, two scholars noted for their pro-British and anti-republican ideology.

350 Ridgeway, J. and P. Farrelly. 1994. The IRA From Belfast to the Bronx. *The Village Voice*, 39:6:29-36.

A journalistic piece stimulated by Gerry Adam's visit to the United States that examines the connections between New York and the IRA. It also attempts to examine the IRA's strategy in sociocultural context. An interesting piece that begs further in-depth research on many aspects of the struggle.

351 Shannon, W.V. 1975. Northern Ireland and America's Responsibility. *The Recorder*, 36:28-42.

An interesting analysis of the sociohistorical factors that have led to the institutionalization of social injustice in the six counties of northeast of Ireland. Written by a former American Ambassador to Ireland, the author suggests a somewhat bizarre three point plan to solve the situation and bring about a united Ireland.

352 ____. 1985. *A Quiet Broker, An American Role in Northern Ireland*. Priority Press, New York.

A very brief personal view of a former United States ambassador to Ireland on the history and development of the situation in northeast Ireland. It is a naive, liberal account that contains no useful insights. It is laced with unsupported anti-republican commentary, and repeats most of the establishments cliches and mistakes about the struggle.

353   Simon, S. 1982. The Irish Issue in America: How Britain is Losing the Argument. *The Listener*, 108:5-6 (December).
A magazine piece written shortly after the hunger strikes that suggests Irish-American activists were beginning to make headway with the press and many legislators on the issue of British withdrawal from Ireland.

354   Stone, J.L. 1987. Irish Terrorism Investigations. *FBI Law Enforcement Bulletin*, 56:10:18-23.
An article emphasizing that in spite of FBI successes against gun running, US nationals continue to try to obtain weapons for use in northeast Ireland. Most of the article consists of a summary of significant activity in the United States and the FBI's response.

355   Thompson, J.E. 1984. United States-Northern Ireland Relations. *World Affairs*, 146:4:313-339.
A well written article that outlines the nature of the American government's approach toward the struggle in northeast from the Nixon administration to that of Ronald Reagan. It also examines some aspects of congressional activity related to the issue. Finally it closes with an examination of the British position but from a rather moderate political viewpoint.

356   ____. 1987. The Anglo-Irish Agreement and Irish American Politics. *Conflict*, 7:3:285-301.
An attempt to analyze Irish-American lobby efforts related to the Anglo-Irish agreement, the International Fund for Ireland and the US-UK supplementary Extradition Treaty. An interesting article using conflict analyses for interest group research. However, the author mistakenly claims that the Irish National Caucus is a lobby group for Noraid.

357   Walker, C. 1979. The American Threat to Ulster. *The Spectator*, 242:11-12 (Feb 3)
            A brief piece on the occasion of a UDA delegation headed by Glenn Barr coming to America to meet US congressmen.

358   Ward, K. 1984. Ulster Terrorism: The U.S. Network News Coverage of Northern Ireland, 1968-1979. In: *Terrorism in Ireland*. Y. Alexander and A. O'Day, eds. St. Martins, New York. pp. 201-212.
            A rather simplistic content analysis of stories on northern Ireland appearing on the nightly news between 1969-1980 on the major American Networks CBS, NBC and ABC. The author comes to the ludicrous conclusions that the British presence was not properly covered and that the IRA's cause is depicted in a positive light. He also accuses American reporters of value judgements while writing an essay that is saturated with the author's own value judgements.

359   Williams, R.M. 1973. American Aid: Lifeblood for the IRA. *World Magazine*, April 24:28-34.
            An article that charges that Irish-Americans are the chief financial supporters of the struggle in northeast Ireland. It is full of the stereotypical characterizations of Irish-Americans who show concern for the oppression of nationalists in northeast Ireland; romanticism, ignorance and sentimentality. It also contains some commentary on Noraid and the National Association for Irish Freedom.

360   Wilson A.J. 1987. Irish America and the 1980-1981 Hunger Strikes in Northern Ireland. *The Recorder*, 2:2:14-31.
            A rather superficial, biased attempt to examine the Irish-American involvement in the hunger strikes by a somewhat naive outsider or an academic with a hidden agenda.

361   Wilson, A.J. 1991. *Irish-America and the Ulster Conflict, 1968-1985*. Loyola University-Chicago, Ph.D. Dissertation.

A poorly written dissertation with strong loyalist sympathies that is characterized by numerous errors of fact. It takes a cynical view toward the history of Irish political grievances. It is also characterized by selective, slanted interpretations of Irish-American involvement in the struggle in northeast Ireland. However the bibliography is useful for tracking references to the struggle in the popular media. A classic example of a Tory revisionist approach to Irish history but without even an attempt to establish a theoretical framework.

362   Wilson, A.J.   1994.   The American Congress for Irish Freedom, 1967-70. *Eire\Ireland*, 29:1:61-75.

An interesting description of the growth and development of the organization that was really the forerunner of the Irish Northern Aid Committee. Wilson feels that its impact was generally small, but did serve to bring the issue of anti-Catholic discrimination in northeast Ireland into the international arena. He also introduces us to James Cahir Heaney, an Irish-American activist from Buffalo, New York and alerts us to the existence of Heaney's private papers in Tonawanda, New York.

CHAPTER 5

REGIONAL STUDIES OF IRISH-AMERICAN NATIONALISM

363   Beadles, J.A. 1974. *The Syracuse Irish, 1812-1928: Immigration, Catholicism, Socio-Economic Status, Politics and Irish-Nationalism.* Syracuse University. Ph.D. Dissertation.

An interdisciplinary study of Syracuse Irish-American experience. It makes heavy use of case studies, a substantial portion of the work deals with Irish nationalist activity in the early 20th century. It reveals the roles of both religious and lay leaders in Irish-American nationalist agitation, propaganda and "mass" meetings of the era. The phenomena of Irish nationalism is discussed in the context of the total sociohistorical experience of the Syracuse Irish-American community.

364   Brundage, D. 1992. After the Land League: The Persistence of Irish American Labor Radicalism in Denver 1897-1905. *Journal of American Ethnic History*, 11:3:3-20.

An excellent article on working class radicalism among Irish-American workers in Denver, Colorado. It considers Colorado as a center of working class Irish nationalism that was egalitarian and internationalist in scope. It also addresses the ideologies of Irish-American leaders such as Father Tom Moloney, Ed Boyce and John O'Neill.

365   ____. 1992. Respectable Radicals: Denver's Irish Land League in the Early 1880's. *Journal of the West*, 31:2:52-58.

A brief article on the blending of middle class values with political radicalism in the Denver branch of the Land League. It highlights the non-sectarian, non-sexist, and anti-clerical position of the Land League in Denver, as well as, its leadership hostility toward the early labor movement. However, its radical ideology on women, the church hierarchy and Catholic-Protestant relations eventually broadened the scope of the Denver labor movement, an enduring legacy of the Land League.

366   ____. 1981. Denver's New Departure: Irish Nationalism and the Labor Movement in the Gilded Age. *Southwest Economy and Society*, 15:10-27.

This study considers the interrelationship of the labor movement in Denver to Irish American nationalist politics. It considers the Irish-American Land League, the new departure policy of Clan na Gael and Davitt's Land League in the context of Irish-American radical working class militancy. The author uses Foner's interpretation of the Irish-American experience, which stresses radical labor militancy rather than conservative labor activism so often associated with Irish workers in the United States.

367   Brundage, D. 1986. Irish Land and American Workers: Class and Ethnicity in Denver Colorado. In: *Struggle A Hard Battle*. D. Hoerder, ed. University of Illinois Press, Champaign, Illinois. Pp. 46-67.

A brief article on Irish labor union activism in the Denver area and its relation to Irish nationalist activity in the area. It contains significant information on the Land League and its class composition.

368   Buckley, J.P. 1974. *The New York Irish: Their View of American Foreign Policy 1914-1921*. New York University. Ph.D. Dissertation.

A historical analysis of the participation of New York Irish in the fight for Irish independence during its most crucial years (1914-1921). It emphasizes the pivotal role of Daniel Cohalan, John Devoy, Jeremiah O'Leary and Robert and Austin Ford, as well as, *The Irish World* and *Gaelic American* newspapers. It also documents the constant attempt to influence American foreign policy on behalf of the Irish people, as well as the Irish-American struggle with Woodrow Wilson in the aftermath of World War I. The struggle for control between Judge Cohalan and De Valera is considered in light of its impact on Irish-American influence. It relies heavily on an extensive examination of the private papers of Irish-American leaders and a survey of the Irish and Catholic newspapers and periodicals of the period.

369   Clark, D. 1971. Militants of the 1860's: The Philadelphia Fenians. *Pennsylvania Magazine of History and Biography*, 95:98-106.
       A brief but well-done analysis of the successes and difficulties of the Philadelphia Fenians in the 1860's. It highlights some interesting connections to the Catholic Church.

370   ____. 1991. Leadership: More Power to Them. In: *Erins Heirs: Irish Bonds of Community*. D. Clark edt. University of Kentucky, Lexington, pp.142-186.
       This chapter contains a brief analysis of two Irish nationalists from Philadelphia: Mike McGlinn and Michael J. Ryan. McGlinn was active in the working class organization, Clan na Gael, while Ryan was involved with the Land League, the United Irish League and other constitutional nationalist organizations.

371   ____. 1982. Martin Ignatius and Dynamite Luke. In: *Irish Relations*. D. Clark edt. Associated University Press, East Rutherford, New Jersey. Pp.114-125.
       Brief biographical sketches of two Irish-American nationalists from Philadelphia: Martin I. Griffin and Luke Dillon. Griffin was involved with the Irish Catholic Benevolent Union and the Land League, while Dillon was involved with the Fenians and Clan na Gael. A good comparison of constitutional and revolutionary nationalism.

372   ____. 1982. John Reilly's Fight Against Partition. In: *Irish Relations*. D. Clark ed. Associated University Press, East

Rutherford, New Jersey. Pp.126-139.

A chronological sketch of the activities of John Reilly of Philadelphia in a variety of Irish organization from the Rising of 1916 to the present day struggle. It contains some interesting observations on his relationship to important issues in the United States and Ireland.

373   Colton, K.E. 1940. Parnell's Mission to Iowa. *Annals of Iowa: A Historical Quarterly*, 22:312-327.

A description of Charles Parnell's trip to Iowa with emphasis on major appearances in Des Moines, Dubuque and Davenport. The author feels that Parnell's visit created sympathies for Ireland and greatly aided the organization of American Land Leagues branches in Iowa.

374   Deacy, J. 1972. The IRA, New York Brigade. *New York Magazine*, 5:11:40-44.

A popular piece written shortly after Bloody Sunday describing the Irish-American community in New York's reaction to the reemergence of the Irish issue. A brief account of the founding of Irish Northern Aid as well as the IRA split into the provos and officials.

375   Delury, J.F. 1986. Irish Nationalism in the Sacramento Region (1850-1890). *Eire\Ireland*, 21:3:27-54.

A brief history of the how, when and why of Irish settlement in the Sacramento region. Discusses a variety of Irish-American organizations in the area and how they served the cause. It includes material on the Fenians, Land League, Irish Republican Brotherhood (IRB), Clan na Gael, as well as, state militia, benevolent associations and relief organizations.

376   Donovan, H.D.A. 1930. Fenian Memories in Northern New York. *Journal of American Irish Historical Society*, 28:148-152.

A very brief account of the Fenian days around the village of Ft. Covington in northern New York during the summer of 1870.

377   Dowling, C. 1982. *Irish-American Nationalism 1900-1916: Butte as a Case Study.* University of Montana, Masters Thesis.

An interesting regional study of Irish-American nationalism in an area not typically thought of having a strong Irish connection. It presents much primary material on Irish-American nationalism in the mountain west. The author however, is obviously influenced in her interpretations by the revisionism so rampant in academic Irish studies today. Nowhere is this more blatant then her forced inclusion of an emotional outburst about Irish-Americans and the struggle today, as part of the conclusion to a study of period 1900-1916.

378   ____. 1989. Irish-American Nationalism 1900-1916: Butte as a Case Study. *Montana: The Magazine of Western History*, 39:2:50-63.

An interesting popular history of Irish-American involvement in Irish nationalism in the early 20th century based on the authors masters thesis. In it, Dowling attempts to show the differences between Irish-American nationalism and Irish nationalism. Her approach is interesting, but somewhat marred by personal value judgements of a revisionist nature.

379   Emmons, D.M. 1985. Immigrant Workers and Industrial Hazards: The Irish Miners of Butte 1880-1919. *Journal of American Ethnic History*, 5:1:41-64.

An excellent article primarily focusing on the work conditions and activism of Irish miners in the late 19th and early 20th century. However, it has a great deal of relevant material on the Robert Emmet Literary Association, Camp 60 of the Clan na Gael.

380   ____. 1989. *The Butte Irish: Class and Ethnicity in an American Mining Town 1875-1925.* University of Illinois, Urbana, Illinois.

An award winning study of the Irish in Butte, Montana, one of the most Irish dominated towns of the period. It contains much material on the Robert Emmet Literary Association or Camp 90 of the revolutionary Clan na Gael. It is a story of the interaction of Irish working class radicalism, Irish nationalism and Irish social mobility and the clash of values such interaction brought. Very well-written, meticulously documented, an enduring reference source and a model for historical studies of ethnic communities.

381   Funchion, M.F. 1973. *Chicago's Irish Nationalists, 1881-1890.* Loyola University, Chicago. Ph.D. Dissertation. (Reprinted 1976, Arno Press, New York)

A sociopolitical study of Irish community in Chicago from 1833-1890 that focuses on the dynamics of Irish nationalism. It is a detailed consideration of the development of Irish nationalism and its interaction with American politics. A most important source on the role of the Clan na Gael, the most important Irish nationalist organization of the late 19th and early 20th century.

382   ____. 1975. Irish Nationalists in Chicago's Politics in the 1880's. *Eire/Ireland*, 10:2:3-18.

A detailed study of factionalism within the Clan na Gael, Irish nationalist participation in local politics and the Irish nationalist influence in the presidential elections of 1884 and 1888. A good source of primary source material for the study of Irish nationalism in the Great Lakes Region.

383   ____. 1981. Irish Chicago Church, Homeland Politics and Class in the Shaping of an Ethnic Group 1870-1900. In: *Ethnic Chicago*. Holi, P.G. and P. Jones, eds. Eerdmans, Grand Rapids. Pp.8-39.

This article considers how the interaction of religion and politics led the Irish to a position of power. It also emphasizes the unifying role of Irish nationalism in the maintenance of ethnicity and how nationalism freely intermingled with Catholicism and local politics. But the author also feels that the respectability associated with political power eventually destroyed the ethnicity of all but a few Chicago Irish.

384   ____. 1987. The Political and Nationalist Dimension. In: *The Irish in Chicago*. L.J. McCaffrey edt. University of Illinois, Urbana. Pp.61-97.

A brief well-documented chapter on the history of Irish nationalist activity in Chicago along with the political aspects of Irish life in the city.

385   Geary, J.W. 1982. Toward the 'Lace Curtain': The Irish in Cleveland in the Immediate Post-Civil War Era. *Ethnic Forum*, 2:60-76.

Another study that illustrates the vast difference between the Irish-American experience in the east and the midwest. It traces the post-Civil War development of the Irish in Cleveland to a position of economic substance. The study raises a number of questions for further study, such as was Irish nationalism really weaker in Cleveland than in other cities, and if so why.

386   Gordon, M. 1977. *Studies in Irish and Irish-American Thought and Behavior in Gilded Age New York City*. University of Rochester. Ph.D. Dissertation

A study of Irish life in New York between 1870-1880 including the role of song and poetry in keeping the collective national experience alive for the Irish. It explores what the author calls the symbiotic relations between Irish-American nationalism and American labor from a philosophical as well as, the organizational viewpoint. The American worker and Irish peasant were exploited economically and culturally by monopolists in both countries. A good companion to Foner's work in Section I.

387   Jeffreys-Jones, R. 1975. Massachusetts Labor and the League of Nation Controversy in 1919. *Irish Historical Studies*, 19:76:396-416.

A detailed analysis of the defeat of the League of Nations which has been often attributed to Irish-Americans. The author, using Massachusetts an Irish stronghold as a test case, feels that the Irish and other ethnic groups were insufficient to defeat the League alone. She feels that peace, prosperity and labor apathy were more significant.

388   Jones, P. 1960. The Philadelphia Lawyer. *Catholic Digest*, 24:4:57-60.
       A brief biography of Michael Francis Doyle, a lawyer from Philadelphia, who was responsible for saving De Valera from a death sentence and later returned to defend Irish patriot Sir Roger Casement against high treason for his part in the Rising of 1916.

389   Jones, W.D. 1967. Made in New York: A Plot to Kill the Queen. *New York Historical Society Quarterly*, 51:311-325.
       The story of an alleged plot to kill Queen Victoria during Fenian times. An orderly room clerk to Colonel Roberts of the Fenians, George Kelly told Canadian Prime Minister MacDonald that he overheard the plans. He said 30 armed men were sailing on a Danish ship for England to assassinate a number of top English including the Queen, the Archbishop of Canterbury, Disraeli and others. Precautions were taken but doubts were raised as to the authenticity of the plot.

390   Kelley, D.J. 1986. Irish-Americans and World War I: An Analysis of the Responses of the Minneapolis Irish Standard. *Hennepin County History*, 45:2:3-29.
       A content analysis of the *Irish Minneapolis Standard* during four distinct stages of World War II, with respect to the nature of the war and its relationship to Irish freedom.

391   Luning, P. 1993. Irish Blood. *Chicago History*, 22:3:21-37.
       Using the controversy over the 1889 murder of Clan na Gael member, Dr. Patrick Henry Cronin, the article discusses the position of the Clan na Gael in Chicago as well as the debate over Irish-American loyalty to the United States. The author concludes that Irish-Americans weathered a storm of nativist criticism related to their zealous Irish nationalism while strengthening their own

ethnicity. Irish nationalism survived the Cronin scandal and devotion to Irish culture was greatly reinforced by the Irish community's examination of their position in America.

392   McGee, R. 1970. *The Fenian Raids on the Huntington Frontier, 1866 and 1870*. R. McGee, Malone, New York.
         A brief monograph that describes the nature of the Fenian raids into Canada along the northern New York frontier. It is very biased toward a Canadian/British viewpoint but provides some interesting local details not generally found in the larger works on the Fenian movement.

393   McGowan, B.K. 1994. *Historical and Ethnic Retention of Irish Republicanism in a Large Midwestern City*. Wayne State University. Ph.D. Dissertation.
         A study of the history and development of Irish republicanism in Detroit, Michigan. It includes an analysis of historical materials as well as interviews with present day activists. It also includes a comparison of the viewpoints of Irish cultural group members with members of Irish nationalist groups such as Irish Northern Aid and the Irish Unity Conference with respect to the present struggle in northeast Ireland.

394   Meagher, T.J. 1985. Irish All the Time: Ethnic Consciousness Among the Irish in Worcester, Massachusetts 1880-1903. *Journal of Social History*, 19:2:273-303.
         A general article on Worcester, Massachusetts that includes significant material on local nationalism, especially the Clan na Gael.

395   Myers, P.E. 1981. The Fenians in Iowa. *Palimpest*, 62:56-64.
         A brief description of Fenian activity in Iowa especially in areas with large Irish populations like Des Moines, Dubuque and Iowa City. It also discusses the role of the Clan na Gael and the Irish Land League in Iowa.

396   Niehaus, E.F. 1965. The New Orleans Irish and Ireland
        1830-1862. In: *The Irish in New Orleans 1800-1860*. E.F.
        Niehaus edt. Louisiana State University Press, Baton Rouge,
        Louisiana, pp. 147-155.
                A brief account of nationalist activity in New
        Orleans from the repeal movement to the Young Irelanders.
        A very biased value-laden account that trivializes Irish-
        American hopes for Ireland.

397   Patrick, J.J. 1983-1984. The Cleveland Fenians: A Study in
        Ethnic Leadership. *The Old Northwest*, 9:4:307-327.
                An interesting study of Fenian Brotherhood in
        Cleveland and its effects on local politics, ethnic identities as
        well as support for Irish nationalism.   It traces the
        development of the movement and its eventual split and the
        effects of the split on the Irish population of Cleveland.

398   Robinson, D. (edt) 1912. Fenians in South Dakota. In:
        South Dakota/Historical Collections, 6:117-130.
                A collection of correspondence regarding the Fenian
        raid on Canada and a brief biographical sketch of Fenian
        General John O'Neill.   Includes correspondence from
        General Winfield Hancock, A.T.A Kerman, Warren Cowles,
        George H. Williams, Doane Robinson, J.A. Fowles and
        General John O'Neill.

399   Roney, F. 1931. *Frank Roney: Irish Rebel and California
        Labor Leader: Autobiography*. Gross, I.B. edt. University of
        California, Berkeley.
                An autobiography of Frank Roney, a Belfastman
        who fled Ireland because of his involvement in Fenian
        activities. He settled in San Francisco and became an active
        participant in the working class struggle against corporate
        capitalism.

400   Rossi, J. 1985. Michael Francis Doyle of Philadelphia.
        Eire/Ireland, 20:2:105-129.
                A brief history of the life of Michael Doyle, a
        Philadelphia lawyer and Irish-American activist. It examines

Doyle's support for Roger Casement in 1916 and his attempt to overturn Casement's conviction for treason. He was also part of the 1919 delegation that asked Woodrow Wilson to place dual self-determination before the Versailles Conference. He also served the American Committee on Conditions in Ireland as counsel and took part in the controversy over the disposition of bond certificates.

401   Sarbaugh, T.J. 1980. *Culture, Militancy and De Valera: Irish-American Republican Nationalism in California 1900-1936.* San Jose State University. Masters Thesis.

An excellent study of the development of Irish-American republican nationalism in California during the years of 1900-1936. The author contends that it was the Bachelors Walk incident in 1914, not the Rising of 1916 that was a turning point for Irish-American nationalists in California. It is a detailed chronology and analysis of a wide variety of republican activity and the impact of personalities from Father Peter Yorke to Joseph Scott and Eamon De Valera. An outstanding contribution to the literature of Irish-American nationalism.

402   _____. 1983. British War Policies in Ireland 1914-1918: The California Irish American Reaction. *San Jose Studies*, 9:1:24-33.

A short but very interesting piece that centers around Father Peter Yorke and the Friends of Irish Freedom activities surrounding the British entry into World War I and the prospect of introducing conscription into Ireland. It also details the dispute between Yorke and Garrett W. McEnerney over Irish-American support for World War I.

403   _____. 1984. Ireland of the West: The Development of Irish Republicanism in California 1900-1916. *Pacific Historian*, 28:43-51.

A well organized introduction to the emergence in California of militant Irish republicanism out of the Gaelic League, after the Bachelors Walk incident in Ireland and the postponement by British parliament of Home Rule .

404   ____. 1990. Eamon De Valera and the Northwest Irish
Nationalism Confronts the Red Scare. *Pacific Northwest
Quarterly*, 81:4:145-151.

An interesting account of a rarely studied issue: De
Valera's American campaign in the Pacific Northwest
between November 7 and November 15, 1919. After a
powerful welcome among Irish-Americans in Butte Montana,
he was denounced in Spokane, Seattle and Portland by the
American Legion as a symbol of un-Americanism and a
foreign threat. Although De Valera was caught up in a sea
of intolerant pure Americanism and anti-communist rhetoric
Sarbaugh recounts how he effectively dealt with the
situations in each locale.

405   Sullivan, L.E. 1982. The Records of the Ethnic Political
Associations as a Genealogical Source. The Associated
Friends of Ireland in the City of Baltimore. *Maryland
Magazine of Genealogy*, 5:23-33.

A good local source of names for the O'Connell
repeal period of the Irish struggle.

406   Sullivan, M.J. 1968. *Hyphenism in St. Louis, 1900-1921:
The View From the Outside*. St. Louis University. Ph.D.
Dissertation, Chapter III.

This study includes an extensive chapter on Irish-
American nationalism in St. Louis at the turn of the century.
It is part of a larger study on hyphenism in time and place.
It is an excellent source of primary material on Irish
nationalism in the midwest.

407   ____. 1971. Fighting for Irish Freedom: St. Louis Irish-
Americans, 1918-1922. *Missouri Historical Society Bulletin*,
65:184-206.

A history of the founding and development of the
Friends of Irish Freedom in St. Louis during the Anglo-Irish
War and up to the Irish Civil War. It includes a thorough
discussion of the League of Nations conflict in the St. Louis

area, as well as, the decline of Irish-American nationalist groups in St. Louis after the signing of the treaty creating the Irish Free State.

408   ____. 1972. Constitutionalism, Revolution and Culture, Irish-American Nationalism in St. Louis, 1920-1914. *Missouri Historical Society Bulletin*, 28:4:234-245.

A discussion of how Irish-American nationalism differed from the national view that constitutionalism had triumphed over revolutionism.   Sullivan shows how nationalists in St. Louis diffused into cultural, constitutional and revolutionary elements.   In St. Louis revolutionary nationalism had deeper roots than constitutional nationalism but the struggle between these two forces became bitter and very divisive.

409   ____. 1976.   The Irish in St. Louis: The Role of Nationalism in the Irish-American Community.   In: *Varieties of Ireland, Varieties of Irish America*.   B.M. Touhill, edt. University of Missouri, St. Louis. Pp.31-40.

A very brief, well-written introduction to the development of Irish-American nationalism in a small midwestern city.

410   Walsh, J.P. and T.P. Foley. 1974.   Father Peter C. Yorke Irish American Leader. *Studia Hibernica*, 14:90-103.

A discussion of some of the selected controversies in which Fr. Peter C. Yorke, an Irish nationalist priest, was involved during the early 20th century.   Yorke was a staunch supporter of Irish freedom and a spokesman for a highly political, aggressive and upwardly mobile working class.   A substantial part of this article concerns Yorke's attack on Garrett W. McEnerney who publicly stated that any support for Sinn Fein in America amounted to disloyalty and treason since Sinn Fein had sought British defeat at the hands of the Germans.   The author also considers how Yorke dealt with his American, as well as, Irish patriotism after the United States entered World War I.

411   Walsh, V.A. 1981. *Across the "Big Wather" Irish Community
           Life in Pittsburgh and Allegheny City 1850-1885.* University
           of Pittsburgh, Ph.D. Dissertation.
                   A study of the regional origins, migration patterns,
           neighborhood and work settings and associational ties among
           Irish Catholic immigrants in Pittsburgh and Allegheny City.
           Especially good on associational life after the Civil War
           including total abstinence, Irish nationalism, land reform and
           militant labor activities. Deals also with the development of
           cultural differences in the Irish community after the arrival
           of post-famine immigrants.

412   _____. 1981. A Fanatic Heart: The Cause of Irish-
           American Nationalism in Pittsburgh During the Gilded Age.
           Journal of Social History, 15:187-204.
                   Walsh examines the theories of T.N. Brown,
           M.Gordon, E. Foner and K. Miller on the origins of Irish
           nationalism. He attempts to test these ideas with data from
           Pittsburgh and comes to the conclusion that the diverse
           reaction of Irish-Americans to Irish nationalism in the late
           19th century is related to cultural antecedents, the
           neighborhood, the work place and participation in Irish
           organizations.

CHAPTER 6

ARCHIVAL SOURCES AND THEIR LOCATIONS

PAPERS, RECOLLECTIONS AND OTHER PRIMARY SOURCES ON IRISH NATIONALIST ORGANIZATIONS; AVAILABLE TO PUBLIC

American Association for the Recognition of the Irish Republic (AARIR)

James E. Murray Papers-University of Montana

John F. Finerty Papers-University of Michigan

Peter Golden Papers-National Library of Ireland

John Byrne Papers-San Jose State Library

John J. O'Reilly Papers- Historical Society of Philadelphia

American Committee on Conditions in Ireland

American Committee on Conditions in Ireland, Interim Report-1921

Evidence on Conditions in Ireland, Albert Coyle Edt.-1921

Memoirs of Dr. Patrick McCarten (with De Valera in America)-1932

W.M.J.A. Maloney Papers- New York Public Library

American Committee on Irish Independence

Frank Walsh Papers-New York Public Library

American Congress for the Unity and Independence of Ireland

John J. Reilly Papers-Historical Society of Pennsylvania, Philadelphia

American Friends of Irish Neutrality

Papers of the American Friends of Irish Neutrality-St. John's University, New York

American League for an Undivided Ireland

American League for an Undivided Ireland Papers-St. John's University, New York

John J. Reilly Papers- Historical Society of Pennsylvania, Philadelphia

Ancient Order of Hibernians (AOH)

AOH Papers- University of Notre Dame

AOH Papers-American Irish Historical Society, New York

AOH Papers-Iowa State Historical Society

AOH Papers- University of Montana

Clan na Gael

Archbishop James Quigley- Archives Archdiocese of Chicago

DeVoys Post Bag- 1948, 1953

Dennis Clark Papers-Balch Institute Philadelphia

Daniel Cashman Memoirs- National Library of Ireland

Daniel Cohalan Papers- American Irish Historical Society

Frank Conlan Papers- Chicago Historical Society

Gaelic American- 1923-25- New York Public Library

John F. Finerty Papers- University of Michigan

Jeremiah O'Donovan Rossa Papers- New York City Public Library

John Devoy Papers- National Library of Ireland

Joseph McGarrity Papers- National Library of Ireland

Margaret McKim Maloney Papers- New York Public Library

Patrick Collins Papers-Boston College Library

McGarrity Papers-Villanova University/New York Public Library

Patrick Cronin Collection- Chicago Historical Society

Recollections of a Irish Rebel- 1929 (John Devoy)

Reverend Donal M. O'Callaghan Papers (1942-73)- American Irish Historical Society

Irish Historical Society

Robert Emmet Literary Association Papers- University of Montana

Roger Flaherty Papers-Chicago Historical Society

T.V. Powderly Papers- Catholic University

William Onahan Papers- University of Notre Dame

Emmet Monument Association

Joseph Denieffe- A Personal Narrative of the Irish Revolutionary Brotherhood- 1904

Fenian Brotherhood

Fenian Raid Papers-Buffalo Historical Society

Catholic University Archives

Jeremiah O'Donovan Rossa Papers- New York Public Library and Catholic University

Patrick Collins Papers-Boston College

John Denvir- Life Story of an Old Rebel- 1910

John Devoy Recollections of Irish Rebel-1929

Margaret McKim Maloney Papers- New York Public Library

John O'Leary Papers- National Library of Ireland

John O'Leary Recollections of Fenians and Fenianism-2 Volumes-1896

John O'Mahoney Papers- Catholic University

General Thomas W. Sweeney Papers- New York Public Library

J.P. McDonnell Papers- State Historical Society of Wisconsin

Library of Congress-Washington

Public Archives of Canada- Ottawa

Public Record Office- London

Fenian Brotherhood 1866-1921- Missouri Historical Society

National Archives- Washington

National Library of Ireland -Dublin

State Papers Office- Dublin

William S. Sullivan Papers-Western Reserve Historical Society, Cleveland Ohio

Friends of Irish Freedom

Bishop Michael J. Gallagher Papers- Archives Archdiocese of Detroit

Daniel Cohalan Papers (1891-1935)- American Irish Historical Society, New York

Friends of Irish Freedom Papers- American Irish Historical Society, New York

J.A. O'Leary- My Political Trials and Experience- 1919

John Byrne Collection- San Jose State University

T.J. Walsh Papers- Library of Congress

William Bourke Cockran Papers- New York Public Library

Peter Yorke Papers-Archives of the University of San Francisco

Irish National Federation of America

Irish National Federation of America Records- American Irish Historical Society, New York

Thomas Addis Emmet-Incidents of My Life- 1911

William Bourke Cockran Papers- New York Public University

Irish National Land League of America

John P. Devoy papers- National Library of Ireland

John P. Devoy-Land of Eire-1882

Michael Davitt- The Fall of Feudalism in Ireland 1904

Irish National League of America

Michael Davitt- The Fall of Feudalism in Ireland 1904

Special Commission Act 1888: Reprint of the Shorthand Notes on Speeches, Proceedings and Evidence Taken Before Commissioners; 12 Volumes-Great Britain 1890

Irish Northern Aid Committee

The Irish People

Irish Progressive League

Peter Golden Papers- National Library of Ireland

Irish World Land League

Devoy's Post Bag- 1871-1928, 2 Volumes (O'Brien and Ryan Edts.)

Irish Nation- 1881-1883, New York Public Library

Irish World- 1879-1883, New York Public Library

United Irish League of America

John F. Finerty Papers-University of Michigan

John Redmond Papers- National Library of Ireland

United Irish Society of Chicago

James Brennan Papers- Chicago Historical Society

Wilson League of Nations Controversy

Bishop Shahan Papers- Catholic University

David I. Walsh Papers- Holy Cross College

Frank P. Walsh Papers- New York Public Library

James A. Healy Collections- Stanford University (Hoover Institute)

John Cardinal Gibbons Papers- Baltimore Archdiocese Archives

John Quinn Papers- New York Public Library

Joseph Tumulty Papers- Library of Congress

Thomas J. Walsh Papers- Library of Congress

William Bourke Cockran Papers- New York Public Library

William Cardinal O'Connell Papers- Boston Archdiocese

William McAdoo Papers-Library of Congress

Woodrow Wilson Papers-Library of Congress

Anthony Griffin Papers- New York Public Library

Patrick Cardinal Hayes Paper- Archdiocese of New York

Charles McCarthy Papers-Wisconsin State Historical Society

Index

Numbers refer to entries rather than pages.
ARC refers to unnumbered entries in Chapter 6.

141